Interview Preparation

Guide to Answer Questions With Confidence and Get Hired

(Tips and Secrets to Be the Best Candidate and Write Winning Resume and Cover Letter)

Lindsey Lore

Published by Rob Miles

Lindsey Lore

All Rights Reserved

Interview Preparation: Guide to Answer Questions With Confidence and Get Hired (Tips and Secrets to Be the Best Candidate and Write Winning Resume and Cover Letter)

ISBN 978-1-989990-66-7

All rights reserved. No part of this guide may be reproduced in any form without permission in writing from the publisher except in the case of brief quotations embodied in critical articles or reviews.

Legal & Disclaimer

The information contained in this book is not designed to replace or take the place of any form of medicine or professional medical advice. The information in this book has been provided for educational and entertainment purposes only.

The information contained in this book has been compiled from sources deemed reliable, and it is accurate to the best of the Author's knowledge; however, the Author cannot guarantee its accuracy and validity and cannot be held liable for any errors or omissions. Changes are periodically made to this book. You must consult your doctor or get professional medical advice before using any of the suggested remedies, techniques, or information in this book.

Upon using the information contained in this book, you agree to hold harmless the Author from and against any damages, costs, and expenses, including any legal fees potentially resulting from the application of any of the information provided by this guide. This disclaimer applies to any damages or injury caused by the use and application, whether directly or indirectly, of any advice or information presented, whether for breach of contract, tort, negligence, personal injury, criminal intent, or under any other cause of action.

You agree to accept all risks of using the information presented inside this book. You need to consult a professional medical practitioner in order to ensure you are both able and healthy enough to participate in this program.

Table of Contents

INTRODUCTION 1

CHAPTER 1: PREPARING FOR THE INTERVIEW 2

CHAPTER 2: OVER THE PHONE INTERVIEWS 7

CHAPTER 3: INTEREST QUESTIONS 15

CHAPTER 4: HOW TO USE BODY LANGUAGE AND MENTAL ATTITUDE TO CONVINCE INTERVIEWERS TO HIRE YOU ... 25

CHAPTER 5: PERSONAL HYGIENE 30

CHAPTER 6: PRE-INTERVIEW PREPARATION: COMPANY RESEARCH 34

CHAPTER 7: TOP INTERVIEW QUESTIONS 44

CHAPTER 8: PREPARE FOR JOB INTERVIEWS.................... 47

CHAPTER 9: EDUCATION QUESTIONS 52

CHAPTER 10: COVER LETTERS 66

CHAPTER 11: BE POSITIVE 72

CHAPTER 12: HOW TO REACT IN A TOUGH INTERVIEW ... 80

CHAPTER 13: HOW TO DRESS UP FOR AN INTERVIEW 89

CHAPTER 14: DRESS TO IMPRESS 97

CHAPTER 15: FIRST IMPRESSION COUNTS 102

CHAPTER 16: FEATURES & BENEFITS, FEAR & GREED..... 106

CHAPTER 17: THE RIGHT ATTIRE 111

CHAPTER 18: WHAT WOULD YOUR BOSS/PROFESSOR SAY ABOUT YOU?... 114

CHAPTER 19: TYPES OF INTERVIEWS 118

CHAPTER 20: SAMPLE RESUME 127

CHAPTER 21: NON-VERBAL COMMUNICATION 133

CHAPTER 22: TOP JOB INTERVIEW QUESTIONS 143

CHAPTER 23: WAYS TO HUGELY BOOST YOUR JOB INTERVIEW SUCCESS RATE 159

CHAPTER 24: PREPARING FOR ROLE-PLAYS AND LAST-MINUTE TIPS BEFORE YOU GO 180

CONCLUSION.. 194

Introduction

A well-organized CV or Resume will get you an interview appointment, but what will determine you're securing the position is the rate of your performance. Your ability to capture the attention of the interviewer and answer his questions correctly and boldly will undoubtedly secure you the job. So, preparation is the ultimate secret that lies behind a splendid interview performance.

No matter your experience, preparation is the master key behind the success of an interview. Every interview condition varies from one company to another, therefore depending on the position applied for and the type of company will depend on how well you should prepare.

Chapter 1: Preparing For The Interview

Just like any important personal or professional endeavors, you need to prepare well for that job interview because it will determine the quality of life that you will have ahead of you. In order to sufficiently prepare for that interview, you need to give yourself a lot of time doing the following first:

Do some research about the role that you are applying for.

Look into the company history and the dynamics of the organization.

Create a personal impression on the current dynamics, trends, and affairs that are long the line of your job sector.

Explore on what the employer is really looking for and assess your personal qualifications.

List down the possible questions that might be thrown at you during the actual interview.

Read this book.

In addition to these, you also need to accomplish the following first:

Do a detailed planning of the schedule and itinerary of the actual interview day. It is important to make sure that you will arrive at the interview venue around ten to fifteen minutes earlier than scheduled. This will give you sufficient time to rest and compose yourself. You have to bring extra cash just in case you need to take a taxi if you got the directions wrong. If possible, print out the map of the office so that you won't get lost. The map can be easily downloaded if you have Internet connection.

On the night before the interview, you need to decide on what you will wear. For details on what you need to wear, read Chapter 2 of this compendium for the tips.

Sleep early on the night before. Get sufficient sleep. That way, your mind will be more alert and you can better perform if your mind and body are one hundred percent awake.

Looking back to your University life, there is an office specializing on giving advice for career track formation. They also help by giving practice interviews. If you can no longer go back to the University to avail of this service, you may do any of the following alternatives:

Anticipate the questions and practice answering them in front of a mirror or with the help of a close friend or a trusted family member. Ask them to give you the most honest form of feedback so that you will know what to improve.

Practice your speaking skills in the non-interview context. When you are talking with your doctor, or with the supermarket cashier, try to simulate the interview situation. These are opportunities for practice because they allow you to speak with people that you are unfamiliar with.

f you find yourself unsuccessful after an interview, ask for their feedbacks and opinions. These will help you draft a list of advice for yourself. This way, you will know what aspects you should change.

If you have the cash, hire a private tutor to teach you how to act in the context of an interview.

Finally, you need to be familiar of the things that you need to bring to a job interview. The following are some of them:

Generally, you need not bring anything aside from your Curriculum Vitae (CV), your cover letter, your job descriptions and specifications, and of course, your personal notes.

Bring the document that serves as your proof that you are invited and scheduled for interview on that day. Usually, this document also lists down the other documents that you have to bring for further assessment. In most cases, employers ask interviewees to bring certificates of examinations and University diploma. These require some time to locate, so you need to make sure that these are well-prepared way before the interview.

It is worth bringing a notebook and a pen. If you need to give a presentation, be sure to bring a backup copy of the presentation even if you have already emailed it to the company way before.

If you have your mobile phone with you, either switch it off or put it to silent mode to avoid the hassle.

Chapter 2: Over The Phone Interviews

An over the phone interview is not less valuable than an interview performed face to face. In today's society taking time to meet with every probable candidate can make the interviewing process take longer and keep companies from filling much needed positions. Many companies have moved their interview process to be compiled of a phone interview followed by a face to face interview. This allows them to move through candidates more quickly but meet with more of them for a more thorough search for the best candidate.

While a face to face interview allows you to use your body language and be charismatic in person, this does not mean a phone interview won't allow you the same opportunities. With an over the phone interview often perspective employers are checking on the swiftness and thoroughness of your responses as well as your punctuality and organizational abilities. If you spend a lot of time searching for answers to questions this will signal the interviewer that you may not be as organized, or even qualified for the position as they thought. This of course is depending on the type of work.

A good and well written resume is no longer enough to gain you interest as a candidate. Telephone interviews are good ways to weed out candidates who are not fully serious about the position, are under qualified, or simply not a good fit. These initial interviews are screening interviews which allow companies to narrow down their candidate search.

From this short list of candidates they are able to narrow down the search to a handful of people whom they would like to meet in person. This is not always the case as there are times a phone interview is the only interview and you could be offered a position without meeting face to face. Again each company and even each supervisor will run their interview process differently.

There are times when a supervisor may call and create what is called an unscheduled interview. These types of impromptu calls never work in your favor and it is best to reschedule the call at a time when you have the ability to be prepared and be in a quiet space. Be polite and express that you are unable to give the call the attention it deserves at the moment and would like to schedule a time when it would be beneficial for both parties. If they are truly interested in you as a candidate they will be willing to schedule an interview.

Scheduled phone interviews will often make their first contact with you through e-mail or by phone and will request a time in which you will be able to speak. In that time you will be able to prepare yourself for your discussion and present yourself to the best of your ability. The goal is to turn a phone interview into a job offer or face to face meeting.

When taking part in a phone interview it is best to still dress the part. The feeling of professionalism will carry through weather you are in person or not. Wearing your pajamas to your phone interview may make you behave in too casual a manner but dressing as though you are attending the interview in person puts you in a similar mindset as though your were meeting your interviewer face to face.

Furthermore, be sure to have a quite and calm place to conduct your conversation. Having a phone interview with background noise can be distracting not only for you but the other person on the line. Interviewing can be especially nerve wracking so having a place which is calm will help you collect your answers with composure.

Keeping a copy of your resume with you will help you refer to the document should your interviewer have questions. Being able to look to your document will allow you to answer more quickly and not allow nerves to rule over your conversation. Consider your resume as your safety blanket because we all have black outs in our thoughts when under pressure or extreme amounts of stress.

Go to your selected place for your interview ten to fifteen minutes early. Get comfortable and allow yourself to be at ease before beginning the call. If you are using a cell phone be sure to have your phone charged and the charger nearby. A notepad to take notes as you are on the phone will allow you to look back over the conversation and ask any questions you may have if given the opportunity.

Ensure you are able to answer the call when it comes in as there are times when companies simply will not provide another opportunity to interview if your windowed time slot is not met. Conducting phone interviews provides companies a larger range of people they can consider as they are more convenient and can take less time in the day. If your window of opportunity is missed the chance is high there will not be an opportunity to make up the interview. This is why being prepared and early to your chosen space is important and gives less chance of missing your interview.

In a phone interview it is a good idea to listen first. This eliminates a risk of talking over your interviewer. This also allows your interviewer a chance to set the expectations of the interview and be the leader. Take notes if you can while listening so that if any questions arise you will be able to refer back to your notes and be thorough in your discussion. Look for ways in which you can make connections. As the interviewer discusses the job you can connect similarities to the job you currently have or ones you have had in the past. Be sure to only speak when a pause is evident or you are asked a question.

Be sure that you are not dry in the mouth as you are unable to make a first impression with your physical body. Drink lots of water the day before and prior to your interview and ensure you have taken a bathroom break to avoid needing one while on the phone. If you have not spoken for several hours, do some voice exercises before your interview to have a clear and understandable tone. Clearing your throat when speaking on the phone can be a distraction and an annoyance to the person on the other end.

Smiling as you speak will make a huge difference in the delivery of your conversation. While it may seem that this is a silly practice, the difference between smiling and having a strait face can be heard. If you do not believe that this subtlety can be detected, do yourself a favor and record yourself speaking the same sentence twice. In one speak the words while smiling and in the second say the words as you would normally. Play both options back and hear the difference in the way the words are spoken.

Smiling as you talk about work you have been involved in, impacts you have had in your previous positions, things which motivate you, and when answering questions will provide a happy and uplifting tonality to your conversation which will be more engaging to your interviewer and show them you are a positive person. Smiling helps in any situation but when you are unable to make a physical impression, this is a wonderful tool which can make all of the difference in securing a second face to face interview or being passed by for the opportunity of a lifetime.

Chapter 3: Interest Questions

What is your all-time favorite game? Whether it's a board game, video game, or sport, what is your favorite?

Sometimes people will refer to life just as one big game. The game looks different for everyone, however, some of us prefer logic games, others would like to be able to win with their sheer physical strength. The type of games that people like to play, and which ones they're good at, can reveal a lot about their personality. State honestly what your favorite game is, no matter what it might be. Provide a why as well. Do you enjoy sitting down and being strategic? Are you someone that enjoys friendly conversation? Share with them what kinds of games bring you the most joy, and which ones you always seem to win as well.

What about yourself would you improve on if you had the chance?

This is somewhat of another sneaky way to try and get you to reveal what your weaknesses might be! This is one that you will also want to be honest about, but try and choose something about your personality, and not your looks. Though you might hate your teeth, hair, body, or whatever else your biggest physical insecurity is, they are focused more on finding out what you think your biggest downfalls are about your personality.

Something we might not like about ourselves is that we aren't confident enough. Maybe we procrastinate, or we are always running late. Frame this in a way that will let your employer know that you are aware of your flaws, but you are working on it the best you can. Here's what you might say:

I would have to say that I dislike how critical I am of myself. Sometimes after I turn in a project I think of all the things I might have done wrong rather than looking towards what I did right. I am learning to improve on this, as most of the time I am too hard on myself and everything usually turns out fine.

What would your ultimate dream job be?

Your dream job might be to lay on the beach and have people pay you to do nothing all day but eat delicious snacks. You can say this if you want, but they will really be wanting to know what type of personality you have. Be truthful and apply it to the job while also refrain from obviously schmoozing them. You might say something like this:

My dream position would be one where I can have creative freedom while also having a team around me that can help support me with my accountability deadlines, or someone that offers creative perspectives when I'm stuck. I would want a changing environment where I could grow, but one that is also reliable that I know I will have around because job security is important to me.

What is the last book, movie, and television show that you watched? What is the last video you watched on YouTube?

This is a question based on your personality and on wanting to get to know more about you. NEVER lie to make yourself sound smarter. It might be tempting to say that you just watched that recently released 3-hour economics documentary, but the person conducting the interview might have just watched that last night and is ready to talk about it in great detail! Ensure that you are being truthful and let your personality shine through. They will get a good sense of who you are and the things you like when you honestly share media that interests you. Who knows what you might legitimately be able to connect with someone on! Never say that you haven't read a book in a while either. Before going into the interview, even if it's something that is totally unrelated to books or TV, have an answer for this one prepared.

What is a personal goal that you have in life?

Your interviewer can already guess that your goals revolve around your career, which is why you are trying to get a job at the moment. What you will want to focus on for this question is not just what your career goals are, but what you might be wanting in your personal life as well. Maybe you want to be a better person, someone that's more giving, a great father/mother, or start to live a healthier lifestyle. This question is non-work related, so share what your personal dreams are! This will help to show that you are focused on excellence and are dedicated to a purpose.

One of my personal goals is to eventually complete a triathlon. I have done various other races, but this is something that I have been working towards for several years. I am hopeful that one day I'll be able to not only finish one but to place in a top position as well!

What kinds of hobbies do you have, or what do you like to do in your free time?

The person conducting the interview is going to start getting more into what kind of things you like to do in your free time. they are curious about the personality traits you have, and what kind of commitment that you partake in. Never say that you don't have any hobbies, and don't let your hobbies be something like, hanging out with friends. Dig deep and find something that you enjoy that makes you happy. You might not consider it a hobby at the moment, but any little trade or craft you have can help them see that you are passionate, dedicated, and responsible. Here's a good response:

I would have to say that one of my hobbies includes cooking. I love trying out new foods and experimenting with recipes as often as possible. I also love gardening and have my own herb garden that I get to experiment with. It's a fun way for me to learn new things and also helps to keep me relaxed in my free time.

Would you rather be a leader or a follower?

The person conducting the interview is going to ask you this because they want to get a sense of the type of person that you will be in their team. Will you be able to be a follower? While it's good to be a leader, you also want to make sure that you know how to take direction and listen when it's appropriate.

If I had to choose whether to be a leader or a follower I would have to say that I'd rather be a leader. This is because I think that a good leader knows that they are supposed to let others lead in certain situations. A leader is not about always holding the highest position of power, but instead, becoming a respectable role model to others that might look up to you. I know when to take the backseat and let others lead while still ensuring that I have control over my own actions.

What is a goal that you have specifically related to work?

This kind of question will be a little obvious to the person conducting the interview, but they want to hear it in your own words. For example, if you were in the business of management, they would assume you want to make it to a higher management position. However, make sure that you are keeping it specific and that it goes beyond just some sort of title that you would like to receive.

I would say that I hope I find a position that makes me a decent living, is fun and fulfilling, and allows me to have enough free time with my family. As long as I can feel like I am doing something good with my time, but also not sacrificing who I really am, then I will feel as though I have achieved the goals of my professional life.

What was the biggest issue you had in your last position? What bothered you the most about your last job?

This is a good question so they know what common problems you might face in the workplace on an individual level.

Interviewers will want to see what parts of a professional setting you might have been dissatisfied with. Many interviewees will be nervous, thinking that it's a trick question as what if you say something negative that this position actually includes! Don't be afraid, they just want to hear some brutal truths from you! Share how you truly felt in your last position but frame it in a way that you are able to also communicate something that is important to you in regard to work values. This is something that you could say:

In my last position, I felt like there was a lack of communication. Sometimes people would misinterpret what I said, and things weren't always expressed as soon as they should have been. I learned what good communication skills were from this position in the process at least.

Who is your role model? Who is your biggest hero?

Your role model will reveal a lot about you. If you pick someone who is close to you, it shows you value the people closest to you on a different level. If you pick someone that is successful, it shows that you have high goals in life. Pick honestly and choose someone you legitimately look up to. Pick a general hero and try to stay away from a political figure or a religious figure.

While they might be a great role model in your eyes, it might be controversial for the person conducting the interview. Though it is discriminatory to not hire someone based on their religious or political views, it would be hard to prove that they did this since they didn't directly ask you the question. Keep it general and pick someone with strong values and respectable qualities. Describe them by their achievements and positive qualities that you think would be important to the specific job that you are applying for.

Chapter 4: How To Use Body Language And Mental Attitude To Convince Interviewers To Hire You

ARRIVING AT THE BUILDING

1) Before entering the building, make sure that you show a positive attitude both inside and outside. Convince yourself that you CAN and WILL pass the interview test. That you are the right person for the job.

Show them that you are excited and eager to work for the company. This is especially important for fresh graduates with little or no work experience. One thing that you can offer to the company, beside your intelligence and skills, is your enthusiasm and your willingness to work hard.

2) Walk with confidence. Convince yourself that you are the best candidate for the job. NEVER ever show negative attitudes and emotions, such as insecurity, fear, doubt, and so on. Now it's the

moment of truth. Be brave, daring and enthusiastic. Keep your spirits high and don't forget to put a sincere smile on your face. Pretend that it's only a trivial thing, a piece of cake and no big deal for you.

3) Upon your arrival, don't forget to introduce yourself to the receptionist, security or other staff there. Tell them that you have come for an interview.

In the Interview Room

1) Enter the interview room with a strong belief that you'll be offered the job. Smile to everyone there and shake their hands firmly. DON'T sit down until they ask you to.

You should answer firmly during an interview. For example, if you were asked whether you were able to do a particular task, you should immediately answer, "Yes!" or "Absolutely!"

2) Sit straight but comfortably and put your bag on the floor. Don't lean on the chair or cross your hands. Don't cross or

stretch your legs. Don't make too many unnecessary moves such as touching your hair or nose, etc.

3) Pay attention and look the interviewers in the eye when they're talking to you but don't stare at them. Listen to their words attentively. Don't look down or look somewhere else.

4) Give a straight, short and convincing answer. Prepare your answers beforehand, if necessary. Don't be too creative by improvising too much. If you are uncertain about a question, ask them politely to repeat it again.

5) Maintain a formal and professional attitude even if the interviewers try to behave informally. Don't try to be funny or be too familiar. Always maintain a good distance with the interviewers. Remember, anything you say or do will be assessed by the company.

6) Don't say anything negative about anyone, including your previous jobs and employers.

7) Be confident, happy and optimistic when talking to the interviewers.

8) Be honest and be yourself. Don't try to be someone else or not yourself to please the interviewers.

9) Never ask about salary, working hours and benefits unless they ask you to. All of these will be explained to you when you are offered the job.

10) At the end of the interview, shake the interviewer's hand firmly and say thank you. Say thank you to the receptionist and other staff outside the room. Don't forget to smile.

11) As soon as you arrive at home, try to remember all of your answers. Where did you go wrong? What can be improved in the future?

The interview is the final stage of the recruitment process. You have picked a job and a company, sent an application letter, and now you are invited to meet the company face to face.

They are interested in you. Don't waste your opportunity! Now is the time to concentrate all of your efforts on winning the job.

Try to see things from the company's perspective. What's in it for them? Why should they hire you? What are your strengths? What can you contribute to the company?

Chapter 5: Personal Hygiene

You can be wearing the best suit or outfit but if you have poor personal hygiene it can ruin the best outfit in the world. You need to make sure that you have a clean and fresh body before you step into your interview. If you do not you will give the impression to your future boss that you are sloppy and careless. On the day of your interview make sure to wash yourself by having a shower or bath, washing your hair too.

Try and do this as close to your interview time as you can. Do not go to the interview with wet hair, make sure to style and dry your hair properly. When you enter the interview you want to look and smell lightly of clean and fresh, this will make you feel good to and this will show when you walk into the interview room.

Give Your Hair some Attention

Don't wear excessive hair products when going for a job interview, make sure that you have properly styled and dried your hair before your interview.

Get a new hair style and cut for interview make sure to avoid anything excessive like spikes, and fancy hair clips make sure that you do not have dandruff before the interview brush your shoulders off

Perfect Nails

When you give your future boss a hand shake they will see your nails right away. If you do not take care of your nails this will lead them to believe that you may not pay attention to the details of the job.

Make sure your nails are dirt-free as a lady you can keep your nails as-is or you may apply a light color of nail polish make sure that your nail edges are nice and even.

Dress for the Job

If you are not certain what type of dress you should wear to the interview ask the interviewer what their dress code is. This will help ensure that you will fit in wearing the right kind of clothes to fit the companies' dress code. Your future boss will think that you fit in perfectly with their work environment.

1. If the job you are applying for is a professional job (such as law, insurance, banking), dress in a professional manner:

if you are a lady you may want to go with a suit and conservative shoes. Try to avoid choosing skirts especially very short ones and high spiky heels.

If you are a man you should choose a dark-colored suit, with long-sleeve shirt, formal shoes, and tie. You should also carry a briefcase this could include male and female.

2. If the job you are applying for is in a business casual environment, such as a laboratory or at a construction site, your dress is going to be different.

For a lady you can wear anything black or grey. Avoid an outfit that is low-cut and has slits. You can wear skirts as long as the hemline is just above the knees, no miniskirts.

For a man you could wear a shirt with a vest or sweater. You can wear V-neck sweaters if you wear a collar. You can wear dress pants, corduroy pants, trousers, but no jeans.

Chapter 6: Pre-Interview Preparation: Company Research

Another surefire way in which to ensure that you are one of the best—if not **the** best—candidate for the position is to demonstrate how well you fit with the company and its culture. This requires that you not only understand exactly what the job is requiring (read and re-read that job description) but also what the company as a whole does and how it conducts business as usual. Showing that you know a good deal about the company—its founding and history, its corporate structure, its products and results, its overall culture—lets the interviewer know that you are a serious candidate with enthusiasm for working at this particular company. This is one of the ways you can set yourself apart from other candidates and set yourself up for success. You want to have a clear understanding of the practical workings of the company, as well as a sense of how workers are expected to behave and produce.

Obviously, review the company's web site thoroughly. This will reveal many truths about a company, from the most basic information to the mission statement to overarching themes that seem to run throughout the organization. You should know all the basic information about a company, such as its history and size. Be sure to read the "About" page on the web site, as it will give you the bottom line regarding a company, but also pay attention to keywords and phrases that come up throughout the site, which will give you greater insight into the corporate culture and specific goals of this particular organization. In addition, the web site's very structure and organization, as well as the quality of its design and writing, will speak volumes about a company—such as whether clear communication or flashy graphics are more important. The same process applies to a company's social media presence: a lot can be inferred about a company based on its presence—or lack thereof—on social media. If there isn't a social media presence, then you can be reasonably confident that the company considers itself traditional or artisanal in some form or fashion. If there is a social media presence, but it is not professionally or consistently run, then you can infer that either the company needs assistance in this area or that its public image is poorly distributed. This is helpful information for you personally, as well as professionally. It would be imprudent to go into an interview with a detailed critique of a company's social media presence, but it might, under cautious circumstances, be a place for you to suggest your worth.

LinkedIn, of course, is the most prominent social media spot for companies and professionals. Do take a glance at that, as well, and if you know the interviewer's name, also be sure to peruse his or her profile in addition. This can give you valuable insight into their specific role within the company and how you can speak directly to that. It can also help with breaking the ice, as well: perhaps you have something in common with the person (school or colleagues, other activities or interests).

Glassdoor is another invaluable site, especially with regard to the interview itself. They offer sets of interview questions and responses that you can peruse, as well as providing reviews from former candidates with information about how interviews were conducted or how companies were operated. These reviews may not always be perfectly accurate—disgruntled employees can certainly vent on this site—but it will allow you to form an overall impression of company culture and practices.

You can also do a quick Google search (Google News is even more pinpointed) to see what is currently going on in the company at large. This is especially valuable if you are applying to a smaller subsidiary or segment of a larger, international company. Basically, you are researching to find out what has been in the news regarding their development and activities in recent months.

Once you've conducted some of this practical research, you can start to spend some time formulating some secondary impressions of the company to give you a sense of how you will fit in and how important this particular job interview is to you. Occasionally, what you might discover in your research will be disconcerting, and you may decide to devote more effort to another position or company armed with that knowledge.

Barring that, be sure that you feel well-informed about the company's strengths. This will be an excellent way to ensure your interviewer that you are enthusiastic about the progress of the company, as well as give you the ability to showcase how your skills dovetail with their strengths.

Take a minute to discern how financially healthy a company is—especially if you are applying to work at a start-up or other emerging company. This allows you to be a better decision-maker, as well as potentially making you an impressive candidate. Knowing some details about the financial dealings of the company can be an advantage in certain cases.

Reinvestigate social media sites with a different goal in mind: how does the company interact with the larger community? Updates about goals and progress, welcoming new customers or divisions within the company, reports about upcoming promotions and events: all of these things will give you a stronger sense of how engaged the company is with the local community, with employees, and beyond. This kind of review can also give you insight into how a company responds to complaints or delays or other problems.

A way to get to know a company in-depth is to seek out someone who works there or once worked there: they will be able to provide direct advice on company culture and goals. Be sure to conduct yourself professionally when undertaking such an attempt—this is for a job interview, not for personal gossip—and know who you are talking to. A former employee may not have the most recent, relevant information, and an unhappy employee may not provide the most accurate assessment.

Do some specific research on the company's history and its top employees, such as the CEO, CFO, and other top management. Name-dropping in an interview can be inappropriate, of course, but you may discover an interesting tidbit that fits perfectly with your own experience. On some occasions, interviewers might expect you to have a working knowledge of a company's founder or historical development. It can't hurt to come prepared.

At this point in your research, you should have been able to glean some information regarding the company's values and how they align with your own. This becomes important with how you will approach certain topics within the interview or hiring process. For example, the subject of work-life balance is always an important one but a sensitive one that should be handled with care. If you notice that the company's values are skewed toward production and shareholders, then you must be willing and ready to put in a long and devoted work week. If the company is devoted to sustainability, then you should be aware of how you present yourself (plastic straws are probably frowned upon). Basically, when you agree to work at a particular company, you implicitly agree with the company's values; be sure that you feel comfortable with and knowledgeable about these core concerns.

While you may not be able to bring up everything you discover in an interview, doing company research has the benefit of preparing you for what to expect, not only during the interview but also when you are successfully hired. Certainly, be prepared to talk about a company's history, mission, and major players, as well as any major achievements that have recently been made. The more that you can present yourself as an already well-informed employee, the better you demonstrate how well you fit into the company culture and its overarching goals.

Last, it also makes perfect sense to spend a little time researching the industry as a whole: knowing what the competition is doing and how they operate can offer ideas as to how you might be able to position yourself as the ideal employee with a breadth of industry-wide knowledge. It can also significantly impress an interviewer if you gain some insight into how your company is responding to particular competition and how you see your presence in that initiative.

Chapter 7: Top Interview Questions

☐Why are you leaving your current job?

☐Can we contact your current employer?

☐Where do you see yourself in 5 years?

☐Have you ever had a bad encounter with a customer? How did you handle it?

☐ Have you ever had a problem with a coworker? How was it resolved?

☐If you knew a coworker was coming in high or drunk, how would you handle it?

☐ Can you tell me a situation where you went above and beyond your job description or duties?

☐ Based on the job description, what do you think you will be doing in this job role?

☐What are your strengths?

☐What are your weaknesses?

☐My son Jason had this type of question on his last interview and shared it with me so I can share it with you.

☐ He said: " You should always be prepared for someone to ask "what would you do if this ____ happened? "Be ready to think fast on your feet on this one, not much preparing you can do as the question may vary. In the past I've had people ask, "what would you do in this high stress situation..." and you need to think of a response quickly rather than freezing up and saying I don't know.

☐ Don't beat around the bush when you answer a question, be direct. People don't want your life story, get to the point. There will be plenty of time to share life stories after you start working with these people.

Some interviews use a point system. X # of points for questions asked, responses given. X # of points for each question you ask them. So back to the page where I said you have a moment when they ask,

"Do you have any questions?" ASK SOMETHING. It may count as a point if you do. Your eye contact, cleanliness, combed hair, all of this gives a point. Be prepared stack those points! Win this interview, you can do it!

Chapter 8: Prepare For Job Interviews

The best interviewees go to the interview well prepared. Approaching the job interview as the single most important step to getting the job, they get ready by reviewing their strengths and goals and also researching the organization. They must anticipate the interviewer and the interview situation and practice strategies to answer anticipated questions with well-thought-out responses. Key questions they need to ask the interviewer must be compiled. Once in the interview, these interviewees try to be spontaneous while still in control of themselves and the interview situation. All else being equal, they interview better than their ill-prepared counterparts because they feel more competent and exude greater self-assurance.

When you conduct an informational interview, you are the interviewer. You now change roles and primarily become the interviewee in the job interview. As you do this, you must follow a new set of rules for effective interviewing. Our best advice: prepare, prepare, prepare. Prepare for the interview as if it were a $1,000,000 prize. Indeed, if you are hired, you may earn that much income during the years you are on the job!

4.1 Conduct Research

When preparing for an interview, you should first research the organization. In addition, try to conduct research on the individual or individuals who will be interviewing you. Obviously, the more you know about the organization prior to the interview, the more you will learn during the interview. You will be a more impressive candidate if you offer thoughtful answers and ask intelligent questions based on the knowledge of the employer. How do you do research on the organization? If you already conducted an informational interview with someone in the organization, you will have acquired some useful information. If you happen to know other individuals in the organization, friends, or acquaintances, contact them for information prior to your interview.

4.2 Information Sources and Questions

Your best information on organizations and the interviewer will come from conversations with people who are close to the organization, especially present and former employees. Hopefully, you have already met with these people in the process of conducting your informational interviews.

4.3 Refocus Your Goals and Strategies

Now it's time to review and refocus your goals and strengths around the specific position you will be interviewing for. This involves more than just generating and synthesizing data on yourself. You must target it on specific organizations and positions. You can begin doing this by first examining any information you have describing the job for which you will interview. Based on both your research and the job description, look for statements of duties, responsibilities, skills, education, and experience as well as any exams required of candidates for the position.

4.4 Practice for Examinations

Many positions require some form of examination as part of the interview process. This may occur at the very beginning as an initial screening device to determine if you should go on to the question/answer stage of the interview. Other examinations may take place after completing the question-answer stage or even during the interview.

4.5 Prepare for Questions

Assuming you know yourself and have done all the necessary research for anticipating the interviewer and the interview situation, you next need to prepare for both general and specific interview questions. Although you cannot anticipate in advance the exact questions the interviewer will ask, you can anticipate the general lines of inquiry. You can expect to be asked questions regarding your education, your work experience, your career goals, and how you get along with others.

Chapter 9: Education Questions

The more recent your graduation, the more intense the interest will be in your education. Because your work experience may be limited, expect to be quizzed for clues to your interests and motivation. For example, how you chose your college and your major (or why you switched), what your extracurricular activities were, any internships you had, and any future career plans (or why you didn't graduate or attend college). Of course, the more your college days recede into the distant past, the less interest there will be in your education. The interviewer can then focus his or her eagle eyes on your work experience.

Why did you choose your major and minor?

These courses were relevant to my chosen career and provided a solid foundation for it.

What the interviewer is asking/looking for: The interviewer wants a sense of your thinking process and interests, and this seems like a good place to start.

Good answer: Give a reasonable reason why. In many jobs, such as computer programming or engineering, it's expected that you majored in computer science or engineering. In other jobs, a wide variety of majors is found in employees. Or perhaps you are passionately interested in the subject, even if it's not "practical." Even if you majored in the Greek and Roman classics, philosophy, or Far East studies, and are interviewing for a job where this is not remotely relevant, be prepared to defend your choice without being defensive. But regardless, be ready to discuss the skills you learned, whether it's researching, writing, communication, or analytical skills.

Bad answer: An answer that shows lack of thought, laziness, or lack of direction. "Because I had to choose something," "It was cool" or "an easy A," or because your parents insisted, your friends were majoring in it, or the workload was lighter than other majors.

What extracurricular activities did you take part in?

I was on my college debate team, arguing topics from ethical to economic issues—and it was a good preparation for my business career.

What the interviewer is asking/looking for: The interviewer wants more of a sense of your interests and how you occupy your leisure time. They hope that you are a well-rounded person who devotes energy and time to something besides your studies.

Good answer: Show that you were interested and involved in things outside school hours—the more these are job-related or show traits the job requires, the better. Perhaps you worked on your college newspaper or yearbook as a prelude to your career in public relations or magazine, newspaper, or book publishing. Or your college basketball games taught you the importance of teamwork and listening to your coach. If you were busy working to pay for college or family bills, with little or no time for clubs or sports, don't be afraid to admit this, noting how you got a jump start on the work world and responsibility over your peers.

Bad answer: Anything that smacks of being a couch potato who simply watched TV or goofed off with your frat buddies after (or instead of) your classes.

Did you have an internship or a cooperative work-study program? If so, what did you learn?

My work-study program taught me a great deal about the field and valuable skills like working with others or research skills, which tie into the job I am seeking.

What the interviewer is asking/looking for: An internship (paid or unpaid) or cooperative work-study program is an excellent way to demonstrate work experience while still in college, differentiate yourself from your peers, and show seriousness of intent.

Good answer: Even if yours was of the coffee-fetching, photocopying, ho-hum variety, highlight the good points, like the chance to actually see and hear how the work was done and network with colleagues.

Bad answer: Bad-mouthing your internship or work-study program, having one in an utterly unrelated field (which makes the interviewer wonder about your real interest in this job), or acting like a smug know-it-all because of your experience.

An internship or cooperative work-study program isn't just a great way to land work experience that looks good on your resume—it may lead to a job. Employers hired 38 percent of their interns and almost 51 percent of their work-study students, a survey of 360 employers by NACE found.

Why are you looking for a job in a field other than in your major?

I enjoyed a volunteer work in this field so much I wanted to switch.

What the interviewer is asking/looking for: The interviewer wants to know your thinking behind your change of direction. Changes of direction are common among young job-seekers—and many older ones as well—but he or she wants to be convinced this job in this field is right for you, now.

Good answer: Make a case on how you looked more carefully at your career goals and the job you are interviewing for is more suitable for various reasons. Perhaps it's a fast-growing field with more opportunity - and jobs for medieval French literature majors were limited. Focus squarely on this job, and relate the skills you developed in your major and any work experience to it as much as possible.

Bad answer: A vague response that reveals you haven't given much thought to your change of direction, and perhaps are taking a scattershot approach to your career planning.

Name an accomplishment during your college years that you are proud of…

I captained the debate team and led it to victory.

What the interviewer is asking/looking for: The interviewer is looking for evidence that you devoted time and energy to setting a positive goal and achieving it, and demonstrated traits or skills which hopefully you will carry over to your career.

Good answer: Anything from an extracurricular activity (at college or outside of college) to a job or volunteer work that shows traits or skills in demand in the work world, such as leadership, initiative, or communication skills. Perhaps you started a campus business making T-shirts, sponsored a child overseas with your parents, or were a candy striper at the local hospital.

Bad answer: Stunned silence, a fumbled response, or anything that tempts the interviewer to think your college years were one long spring break (or that the movie Animal House was modeled after your college experience).

Be sure to dress appropriately and act professionally during the interview, even if the company has lots of young, casually dressed employees. Young job-seekers often are casually dressed in T-shirts, flip-flops, and shorts; answer their cell phones; and pepper interviews with words like "cool," "awesome," "you know," and "like," hiring managers complain.

If you had it to do over, what college courses would you take?

Marketing and public speaking.

What the interviewer is asking/looking for: The interviewer hopes your answer will show your understanding of what the job will require, and include a relevant course or two.

Good answer: Naming courses relevant to the job at hand, in terms of knowledge or skills. For example, marketing, statistics, journalism, or public speaking courses are good answers, if you can make a case the job requires this subject matter or skills.

Bad answer: Anything that shows a complete change of direction from the major you chose, or courses irrelevant to the job at hand, like Chinese art history or philosophy.

Why did you choose your college?

Because it offered a particularly strong program in my field of interest.

What the interviewer is asking/looking for: He or she wants to see anything that shows seriousness of purpose and solid decision-malting ability.

Good answer: Perhaps your school features outstanding professors with time for their students.

Bad answer: Anything that confirms the interviewer's worst fears that you chose your school for the chance to party nonstop without your parents around, because it was the only school that accepted you, or you were forced into it because your father or mother went there.

How do you keep learning? (Or: How do you stay informed?)

I read a local newspaper and at least one business publication, such as The New York Times every day.

What the interviewer is asking/looking for: The interviewer wants to know if you are a professional with an inquiring, curious mind who strives to keep up with information and update your skills. Continuing education has never been more important than today, since technology and globalization have changed every industry.

Good answer: You regularly read trade publications in your field to keep on top of what's happening in your industry. Perhaps you also belong to a professional association, attend its conferences, meetings, or workshops and read its newsletter, take a class to learn a new skill or even a graduate degree like an MBA at night, or teach a class or speak at conferences in your field.

Bad answer: Anything that implies you stopped learning when you finished school, perhaps have not cracked a book open since then, have closed your mind to new things, and get all your information from TV.

Why didn't you finish college? (Or: Why didn't you go to college?)

I had to drop out due to lack of money but I'm willing to finish it within a few years.

What the interviewer is asking/looking for: The interviewer hopes you had a solid reason, as opposed to lack of interest in learning or discipline.

Good answer: If there was any extenuating circumstance, like needing to support your family, or health problems, by all means say so. If you are currently completing your college degree, or plan to, admit it, since this shows you realize its importance. Many people who didn't finish college, stopped after a while, or didn't attend right after high school go later in life when the timing is better, and sometimes go on to earn graduate degrees, including law and medicine.

Bad answer: An answer that shows insufficient interest in learning, displays the inability to focus or discipline yourself for very long, or leads the interviewer to wonder if you knew why then or even now.

Why did you leave college and return later?

I chose to work full-time for a while to gain solid work experience and money to complete my degree.

What the interviewer is asking/looking for: The interviewer hopes to hear any good explanation for your stop-out.

Good answer: Perhaps you traveled, which you found an invaluable learning experience, devoted time to caring for your family, or simply needed to explore your interests and focus your goals more clearly.

Bad answer: You can't articulate a reason for either why you left or why you returned, or say you simply wanted to party a lot.

Summary

You've learned your college days can reveal a lot about you, so treat them as you would your work experience. Be ready to give examples of how you demonstrated communication skills, leadership, a strong work ethic, and other things that employers value highly. Don't be surprised if your employer wants to know how you keep learning, even now.

• Tie in subjects you studied, your accomplishments, and extracurricular activities to the job at hand as much as you can.

- Talk about what you learned from internships and part-time, summer, and work-study jobs.

- Dress, speak, and act professionally in the interview.

- Give a good reason for bad grades or leaving/ not attending college, if that's the case.

Chapter 10: Cover Letters

Office Team, one of America's largest staffing companies, polled executives in 2012, asking each whether they found cover letters to be valuable in evaluating job applicants. Nine out of ten responded favorably, and 80 percent noted that it were common for applicants to submit cover letters — even when a resume is submitted electronically. While it's true that not every individual in charge of hiring wants or reads cover letters, think of it this way: You've lost nothing by sending an impressive cover letter even if it goes unread, but if you don't submit these to the companies that do value them, you'll be working against your chances of having your resume considered. In general, job applicants should consider writing cover letters an integral part of applying to jobs, one that's just as important as writing a solid resume.

Applicants sometimes understand the importance of writing a cover letter but aren't clear on the exact purpose of the document. It should not be a rehash of the resume since there is little point in sending the same information twice. The cover letter should, instead, show that you are interested in the specific position you are applying for, introduce your personality, and give a sample of your written communication skills. A great cover letter will do all of these things in a manner that isn't dry, stuffy, or boring. Much like a resume, a cover letter is a marketing document, one that should ideally make you stand out from the crowd.

You can accomplish each goal of the cover letter using a standard formula, which contains four parts: a header, the introduction, the argument, and the conclusion. Although it might be tempting to stray from this formula in favor of a more unique or creative take, doing so is often a considerable gamble, unless you work in a creative industry such as graphic design. If you craft your words carefully, always keeping your audience in mind and avoiding clichés and repetition, your writing will convey your individuality and intelligence — even though you've used the same formula as every other job seeker. As with writing a resume, you want to tantalize a potential employer into reading further; keep this thought in mind as you put together your cover letters using the four parts below.

The Header

The header includes your information, the company's information, and the greeting:

The Introduction

The quickest way to land your cover letter in the trash is to include a generic introduction, or even worse, to use an opening paragraph that is obvious or trite (e.g., "My name is so-and-so. I am applying for your position as a yo-yo research specialist."). A better way to start is to show your interest in and knowledge of the business — and how you can contribute. Although you may need to spend some time researching, you'll be perceived as a job candidate who understands the position and company, one who is most likely willing to take the time to address its needs. You might write, for example, "I grew up playing with ABC Yo-Yos — I was the first on my block to have the SuperSpinner model — and as a yo-yo research specialist, I'd be proud to design ABC Yo-Yos for the next generation of children to enjoy." This example shows that the writer is involved with the company and can help the company accomplish its goals (designing yo-yos for young consumers).

Using this approach, you will need to write a different cover letter for each job you apply to, but the time spent will set you apart from an army of cut-and-paste robots. Changing your cover letter for each job will also allow you to customize your tone. Whereas it may be okay to use friendly, conversational language when applying to a tech start-up, you would not be wise to do so when applying to a company with a more traditional atmosphere, such as a bank. No matter which tone you choose, however, avoid slang and inappropriate language, which could give the impression that you are unprofessional.

The Argument

After you've written an introduction of about two to three sentences that briefly shows you understand the position you are applying for, and why you deserve the job, it is time to back your claims up with facts. If, for example, you are applying for a sales position, give concrete reasons why you would be a fantastic addition to the sales team. You might give figures from your past sales history, mention whom you've mentored under, or highlight courses you took that relate to the position. Be careful not to use generic statements, such as "I am a hard worker." The person in charge of hiring has no idea whether he or she should believe you, so opt for facts, not unsubstantiated claims.

As you present each piece of evidence, you should relate it back to how it is going to help the company: "Your school has a reputation for encouraging student engagement in extracurricular activities. While studying at XYZ University, I pursued upper-level study in extracurricular involvement, and I would love to use my skills and ideas to boost your student enrollment in these activities." This will also give you the chance to highlight the best parts of your resume, and by relating it to the company's needs, you will avoid the trap of simply restating the information.

Chapter 11: Be Positive

A. Using Positive Visualization to Succeed in Job Interviews

It's typical to be anxious before a prospective employee meet-up — as it would turn out, it isn't consistently that a brief discussion with a close more unusual can possibly change the course of your profession. That said, for some employment seekers these nerves go past insignificant "butterflies in your stomach," and they turn out to be so dreadful and troubled that they get tongue-tied, talk an excess of or say the wrong things.

There are various reasons why you may be in an awful disposition amid a meeting. Possibly you are baffled with your pursuit of employment, or don't feel that the occupation for which you are talking is an awesome fit.

Perhaps you essentially had an awful morning. Yet regardless of how negative you are feeling upon the arrival of your meeting, it is critical not to give it a chance to show.

A positive, amicable mentality goes far in inspiring a superintendent.

Employers want to hire people that appear upbeat and likely to get along with their bosses, co-workers, and clients. Regardless of the possibility that you are all around fit the bill for a position, a negative state of mind can hurt your possibilities of landing the position.

Here are tips for passing on an uplifting disposition amid a meeting – regardless of the fact that you are not really feeling that positive.

B. 10 Tips for keeping it Positive during a Job Interview

1. Dress the Part

When you look great, you feel great. Remember this when selecting your meeting outfit. Take the time to iron your shirt and slacks, clean your shoes, get your hair style – whatever will make you feel certain strolling into the meeting.

2. Think Positive

In the event that you go into a meeting feeling that you won't land the position, or that you will hate the job, it will be hard for you to convince the employer otherwise. Along these lines, before you stroll into the superintendent's office, take a couple of minutes to recall a period when you were effective – whether it was a time when you got a job you wanted, successfully ran a volunteer event, or simply played a great round of golf.

Strolling into the meeting with a positive picture of yourself will help you to pass on a certain mentality to the manager.

3. Focus on Posture

Posture is an important nonverbal form of communication that conveys how you feel about yourself. In the event that you slump or dismiss your body from the questioner, you may appear to be detached or ailing in certainty. Rather, stand up straight (or sit straight) with your shoulders back, and look at the executive without flinching. This stance will make you seem certain even before you say a word.

4. Be an Active Listener

If you are feeling negative during an interview, you might become so bogged down in negative thoughts that you struggle to focus. Rehearse dynamic listening to verify you stay concentrated on the questioner and comprehend what she is stating. Look at the questioner without flinching while she is talking, ask elucidating inquiries, and rethink what she says to guarantee seeing ("So, what you're saying is..."). Active listening demonstrates that you are engaged and interested in the job.

5. Convey a Can-Do Attitude

Regardless of the possibility that you have an inclination that you are not an immaculate fit for an occupation, you would prefer not to underscore that amid the meeting. Prior to the meeting, draw up a rundown of your qualities and encounters that identify with the occupation prerequisites as expressed in the employment posting. Along these lines, if the questioner inquires as to why you're a solid match for the employment, you have various reasons and cases convenient. Regardless of the fact that the questioner inquires as to whether you have involvement with an errand of which you don't know anything, concede your absence of experience, and however underscore your advantage and eagerness in discovering some new information. While having the right stuff essential for an occupation is critical, a positive, can-do state of mind goes far.

6. Smile

Smiling, even when you are not actually feeling happy, can actually brighten your mood. So even if you are feeling disheartened about your job search, walk into and out of the office with a smile. It will put both you and your interviewer in a good mood.

7. Try not to overdo it

Obviously, being forcefully neighborly can likewise be off-putting for a questioner. The questioner needs to see that you are a genuine individual — and genuine individuals don't grin constantly. On the off chance that you utilize this counsel with some restraint, you will appear to be sure and certain, without being overpower.

The primary rule of employment talking is to venture a good picture of you. The second lead is to always remember the first. While the accompanying tips may appear glaringly evident, questioners say that occupation seekers regularly bumble over the same bumbles.

8. Important experience.

At the point when asked whether you've had straightforwardly related experience, say "yes" on the off chance that you have and refer to accomplishments demonstrating it. If not, don't simply say "no." Instead, remark that once in a while are two occupations indistinguishable inside and out, and that you are extremely keen on the occupation and give illustrations of how you took care of regular issues —, for example, cutting expenses, managing displeased clients, overseeing troublesome collaborators — that uncover your reasoning procedures, abilities, and skills.

9. Group connections.

At the point when examining activities on which you lived up to expectations, the questioner may be listening to see whether you go past assuming reasonable acknowledgment for your achievements — would you say you are a credit pig? How regularly do you utilize the credit-getting pronoun "I" contrasted with the group playing pronoun "we." Credit pigs may be not able to execute as colleagues.

10. Flight reasons.

Grumbling in insight regarding why you need to leave your present employment uncovers your qualities, raising suspicions that another position would simply replay your disappointments. Will you ever be fulfilled or would you say you are a grouch?

Clue: Record your responses to potential prospective employee meet-up inquiries. The following day, put yourself on the opposite side of the work area: Listen for what questioners may be hearing. Do you sound like a winner?

Chapter 12: How To React In A Tough Interview

Today there is many different tactics being used during job interviews. Interviewers like to do things such as measure how you react to criticism to using forms of intimidation on you. The trick is for you to be prepared for some of these curve balls that may be thrown at you during a job interview. Below are a few examples that you may encounter.

1) **Fast Speed Interview.** Just because your interview only lasted a very short period of time is not a reason to be worried this does not necessarily mean that your interview did not go well but that the future boss is busy. Many companies are using the speed interview more and more. Studies have shown that the first impression is made within the first 7 seconds of a meeting.

2) **Questions for Them.** Make sure that you do have a few questions for your interviewer, as they will be judging you to see if you did your homework on the history of the company. A good question to ask is "What are the biggest challenges facing the company today?" Also check to see if the company has recently released some new products and discuss them briefly in the interview.

3) **Innocent Inquiries.** When the interviewer asks questions about your personal life such as what your hobbies are they are trying to find out what your personality is and if you would be well suited or not for this job. Don't be too enthusiastic about discussing your personal life, keep answers brief and try not to discuss much about it during your interview.

4) **Asking Questions on a Hypothetical Situation.** This is one of the favorite types of questions that interviewers like to ask which is to give you a hypothetical situation in the job and then ask how you

would handle that situation. An example of this would be "What would your reaction be if a team member was not contributing to a project?" A good answer to this question would be as follows:

"Unfortunately, I have found myself in a similar situation before, I would first try to communicate with the team member honestly. I have found that by ignoring the problem does not make it go away but it just makes it worse. Approaching and speaking to the individual team member in a non-confrontational way is the best approach. Often it is just a lack of understanding what their individual contribution to the project is supposed to be. By approaching it in this manner I am able to find out exactly what the problem is and how to work out a solution."

5) **Discussing Salary Early.** Usually the interviewers wait until later in the interview before discussing salary. If they do bring it up early you can request that you discuss salary later once it has been decided if you are the right candidate for

the job. You could also put a number out there making sure to shoot hire on the pay scale for the job. You can also look up what the standard pay is for similar jobs on sites such as Salary.com.

6) **Weakness.** If the interviewer wants to know what your weakness is remember to be honest because they want you to show that you are able to admit where you need improvement.

Scare Tactics. They could try and use scare tactics on you by doing things like not smiling at you during the interview. They may take their time asking and answering questions. These are things that you do not have control over during an interview but you do have control over how you react to them. Remember to answer the questions clearly and take deep breaths between answers and keep your feet planted firmly on the floor, Do not start to play with your hair or bite your nails or wriggle around in your seat these are classic signs of anxiety. These will not make a good impression during the interview.

Common & Uncommon Interview Questions

Interviews are something that most of us would rather not go through at all but if we want a chance at getting our dream job or at least a career move in the right direction we must endure interviews. But this doesn't mean that we shouldn't get ourselves prepared for questions that we may be asked during them. Also to help us prepare for the ones that we were totally not expecting. This is becoming a more common tool used in interviews with companies such as Google and Amazon; it is said that someone was asked during a Google interview "how many cows are there in Canada?" The interviewer wants to try and gain what your values, character and see how your thought process handles the unexpected. It also gives them a chance to see how you perform under pressure. Below are some of the more common questions given in an interview.

1) What are your strengths?

2) What are your weaknesses?

3) Why are you interested in working for this particular company?

4) Where do you see yourself in 5 years?

5) Why do you want to leave the current job you have?

6) Why was there a gap in your employment?

7) What can you offer the company that someone else can't?

8) What are three things that your former employee would say you need to improve?

9) Would you be willing to relocate?

10) Would you be willing to travel?

11) What is an accomplishment of yours that you are most proud of?

12) Tell me about a mistake you made?

13) What is your dream job?

14) How did you hear about this job?

15) What would you like to accomplish in the first 30 days you are in the job?

16) Discuss your resume

17) Discuss your educational background

18) Describe yourself

19) Describe how you handled a difficult situation

20) Why would we hire you?

21) Why are you looking for a new job?

22) Would you work holidays or weekends?

23) How would you handle and irate and angry customer?

24) What are your salary requirements?

25) Give an example when you went above and beyond the requirements of a project you were working on

26) Who are our competitors?

27) What was your biggest failure?

28) What motivates you?

29) What is your availability?

30) Who is your mentor?

31) Tell us about a time that you disagreed with your boss

32) How do you handle pressure?

33) What is the name of the CEO?

34) What are your career goals?

35) What gets you up in the morning?

36) What would your direct reports say about you?

37) What were your boss's strengths and weaknesses?

38) If I talked to your boss what do you think they would say your weaknesses are?

39) What are your hobbies?

40) Would you work 40+ hours a week?

Hopefully the questions listed above will give you a bit of an idea on the type of questions that you can expect to be asked during an interview but remember there could also be those unexpected questions such as "how many window panes do you think there are in New York city?" Just try and stay cool and calm and give the question a good think over before answering. There is really no right answer for a question such as this they just want to see how you will react and handle this type of question from left field so to speak.

Chapter 13: How To Dress Up For An Interview

Dressing for an interview is a very crucial part in getting your dream job. Yes, this has been long established by professionals from all over the world and has been a conundrum, but still a lot of people are having a hard time dressing properly during an interview. The rule of thumb here is to blend in, but at the same time stand out, which can be quite challenging. It seems superficial to judge someone by the way they dress, because people would want to be measured through their credentials and not through what they wear.

Like how the old saying goes, first impressions last and it is something that has been long proven. The moment you step inside the interview room and before you even say anything, the interviewer has already measured you based on how you look and how you carry yourself. Avoid experimenting for your interview outfit and just make sure that you dress appropriately to the job/field you are applying for and avoid underdressing or overdressing.

Experts suggests that you do some research on the company and its atmosphere, try to check how people dress so that you'd get an idea on what is the appropriate attire in at their workplace.

Here are some DO's and DONT's when dressing for a job interview:

Woman

DO'S

-Always wear clean and ironed clothes.

-Wear buttoned shirts only leaving the one or two buttons open, but make sure that your chest aren't showing.

-Do make your hair clean and simple, nothing too fancy.

-Wear traditional fabrics, such as cotton. Do not wear fabrics like satin and leather.

-Wear conservative shoes that are also comfortable.

-Make sure that you have emptied your pockets, you don't want those keys and loose change to be bulging.

DON'T'S

-Don't wear too much make-up

-Avoid wearing loud colors, such as neon colors. You can use them for accessories, however use them sparingly.

-In any given cases, do not wear jeans or a t-shirt.

-Don't use a strong scented perfume, something mild will be more appropriate.

-Don't wear sandals.

Tips:

-If you're applying for a creative job post, such as a writer, don't be too flashy. Keep it toned down. Yes, you want to show that you have personality, but not "too much personality". Try to show your personality, with subtle accessories and safe colors.

-For client-relations job such as, law firm, sales, marketing or real estate. Keep it simple, invest in a nice blazer that you can use over a simple blouse, no heels higher than 3-inches, shoes should also be closed and keep colors in neutral and nothing too vibrant.

-For a fashion job, such as a fashion designer, stylist, or retail sales. Wear a nice pair of shoes, a nice accessory which will be the focal point of you attire and a nice bag that will display your good taste. It doesn't have to be flashy or expensive. It should reflect your style. You don't want to come off as "too fashion-forward". Wear good clothes that will reflect that you have knowledge on fashion.

-For a finance job, such as banker, stock broker or consultant. Simple advice, conservative and professional. I suggest that you wear a two-piece pant or skirt suit in a dark color. Closed shoes with heels, but not too high.

Men

DO'S

-Always carry a blazer for a more formal look

-Make sure that your shirt and tie are well coordinated with the color of your suit.

-The shirt cuffs must only be shown slightly ion the wrist.

-Make sure that your suit and pants are freshly pressed and it is tailor fitted.

-Your shoes should be polished.

-Socks should match with the suit.

-Get your hair trimmed before the day of the interview.

- Get a clean shave.

DONT'S

-Un-tucked shirts look messy and unprofessional.

-Dress shirts and khaki pants shouldn't go together.

-Don't wear any body piercings, such as earrings or nose earrings.

-Do not wear any type of hats or sunglasses.

-Do not wear any chains. A simple watch would be fine.

-Athletic shoes are inappropriate.

Tips

-Small details matter. Make sure that you show proper grooming on the day of the interview, make sure that you hair is trimmed and your hands and nails are clean and clipped. If you cannot do the extra effort for the interviewer, how would you do it for your boss?

-Blend in rather than standing out. Conform to the look of the office, do a bit of research. Adjust your attire to the working environment. Show your uniqueness through your work ethics.

-Tailor fit your look by investing in a good pair of suit. Make sure that your suit fits you perfectly, not too big or not too small. You'll eventually notice the added confidence of wearing a nicely tailored suit. People can easily notice if a guy's shirt doesn't fit well.

-Be friendly to the receptionist, because good manners can go a long way. Good looks and nice clothes would mean nothing with a rude candidate. Partner your nice attire with the right set of manners. Be friendly to the receptionist, they might just be able to help you.

Judging a person from the way they dress might sound subjective to some, however, when it comes to selecting a candidate it plays a big part. A psychologist once noticed that when an individual posses one desirable trait, that individual is assumed to have more desirable traits too.

Clean and proper attire will give you a positive light and your interviewer may even forgive you for any minor errors you make. When you are in doubt always dress conservatively, sexy shouldn't be an option, especially for the ladies. Jewelry should be kept at a minimum. Another important factor that most candidates seem to look over are the small details. Loose or baggy clothing can make someone look sloppy. Experts say that if a person isn't dressed well, but says the right things, will not guarantee him the job. Just remember to dress well and speak well.

Chapter 14: Dress To Impress

Dressing for any occasion can be pretty hectic, from finding the perfect outfit to accessorizing, whether it's a casual meeting or an interview. People always tend to freak out when it comes to an interview and wreck the whole outfit for looking perfect, but it can be as easy as getting ready for any other day or occasion. By taking a few precautions and dressing appropriately for the interview can let you interviewer know that you take your work and yourself seriously. Dressing appropriately sets a vibe for you. It raises your confidence and sets a tone for the day. It starts off a mood, helps you focus and concentrate as it indicates that you respect standards of the workplace, and are willing to regulate. Being presentable will help elevate your confidence levels and at the same time, set off the right tone with your interviewer. Workplace dress codes have become quite lenient in the past few years, but until you have truly identified with the place, it is better to keep it formal. Following are a few pointers to keep in mind:

Personal Hygiene

Ever sat next to that guy who always smelled of ham and turkey sandwich in the bus? Did you have to write a letter to the company's head requesting a ban on coffee because the coffee stains on the receptionist's teeth really put you off? Nobody wants to sit next to a person with poor hygiene, and nobody would really hire anyone that no one would want to work with. Did you make the connection? Case in point, don't be the person with poor hygiene. We all know that sometimes less can be more, and that is definitely the case when you're headed for an interview. We're all guilty of sometimes going overboard when going for an interview to land that dream job, but it's best to hold your horses. Wearing an excessive amount of perfume is not only inappropriate for a potential workplace, but it can also be impolite and cause inconvenience for the interviewer. Avoid wearing chunky jewelry as it can be distracting and will take away the attention from your professionalism and skills.

·Floss, brush your teeth, and use mouthwash.

·Take a shower and put fresh underwear on.

·Trim and manicure your nails

·Keep the makeup natural. Avoid bright, heavy layers of makeup

·Comb your hair and style them in a stylish and professional manner.

·Wear breathable clothes to avoid sweating excessively.

·Avoid smoking prior to the interview. Even if you do, keep mouthwash or mouth freshener to clear up the smell.

·Keep the perfume minimal.

·Dispose of any chewing gums before going in for the interview.

How to Dress Appropriately

A dress that may be appropriate for an interview at a publishing house may not seem presentable at a law firm. How you dress should be a combination of your own personal style and the industry and place you are applying at. Following are a few do's and don'ts to keep in mind:

Opt for a tailored suit or dress. You don't necessarily have to stick to monotones or neutral colors. You can opt for small prints and some vibrant colors like canary yellow and ink blue. They give off a livelier and more positive vibe. However, avoid going to the interview wearing large prints in neon colors that take the attention away from you.

As with all occasions demanding you to be fashionable and classy, a well-tailored black dress will not fail to impress. Take your documents in a sleek folder. Avoid carrying a large handbag with you, and always keep the bag on the floor next to you. Never put it on the table, and never place it in the way of the foot flow. For men, either take a folder or a briefcase with you. Avoid carrying both. Cover tattoos and if you have a lot of piercings, maybe keep some of the more distractive rings at home. The color of your socks should either be similar to that of your pants, your shoes, your tie or pocket square. If you are wearing a dress, opt for a pantyhose. There are no strict rules, but if someone old school is interviewing you, they will give you extra points right off the bat.

When it comes to shoes, prefer closed-toe pumps with a small heel. Heels just give off a more professional, tailored look. Avoid wedges though as they look clunky and casual. Do not wear flip-flops to a job interview, no matter how casual the dress code is.

For men, avoid sandals and snickers and stick to formal boots in prime condition.

Chapter 15: First Impression Counts

We have mentioned that dressing up makes an important first impression. First impressions are key in establishing impressions because once formed, they are not easily erased and people will use that impression as a basis to judge you in future engagements. In addition to dressing appropriately, here are 5 ways to make a great first impression and set yourself in the right light:

1) Show up on time – You've probably heard this a million times, but no matter how many times you have heard it, it is worth a mention simply because of its importance. If you indeed running due to some unforeseen circumstances, call your interviewers as soon as possible and explain the reason. It's better to let them know that you will be late before the start time of the interview rather than after 30 minutes of wait.

2) Shake hands – When you first meet the hiring manager, make sure that you shake their hands as you exchange greetings. Try not to nod your head or wave your hands as a replacement for a firm handshake (if you have really sweaty palms –wipe your hands before entering the room). A handshake is a sign of goodwill and it also offers a chance for you to show your confidence in moving on.

3) Posture is important –Resist the urge to slouch or hunch over as you summarize your skills set. Slouching can convey that you're sloppy — or worse, that you don't really care about the interview. As silly as it may seem, you may want to practice your sitting style before you get into the interview, to ensure that you sit up straight the entire time.

4) Remain composed – It is quite likely that your interviewer will ask one or two questions that is meant to stump even the most confident interviewers. Examples of the question can be, "Recommend the best strategy for the company going

forward to achieve X% amount of growth year over year." When encountered with questions like these, do not let your nervousness show. Avoid using words like "uhh" or "umm" because it will not look professional on your part.Instead,you can buy a few extra moments of thinking time by saying, "That's a great question," and then go on and talk about your answer.

5) Do something that sets you apart – This is where things might get a little fancy. If you truly want to impress employers and set yourself apart from the rest of the candidates, create something that is unique and impressive. One way to do this is create a proposal for a project relative to the position you're interviewing for. For example, if you're applying for a consulting position, create a mock-up business plan you have written for a prospective client of the company. This is very good way to show your skills and display to the employer your eagerness to land the position. It is always a good idea to run your final product by a friend or family

member. You want to make sure that you are not overdoing your presentation. Before you start to talk about what you have done, always ask the interviewer if he/she would like to see it. Never force it down their throats if they politely rejects your proposal.

Chapter 16: Features & Benefits, Fear & Greed

I want to pause our discussion of the sales process for a chapter to talk about two fundamental concepts of sales that impact the way you ask and answer the questions in the interview.

Features & Benefits

When I was starting out in financial sales I had a boss that would hammer the concept of features and benefits into our brains. After many sales calls he would tell me that I talked ad nauseum about the features of a particular investment product and I spent very little time talking about the benefits.

You see, the problem with this is that for most people features are boring. In television sales the features are things like screen width, is it internet compatible, what types of input and output portals are there? How heavy is the tv? Ultimately, the consumer doesn't care about any of these. What they want to know is will their devices work with the tv? Will it be hard to set up? Will their friends be jealous and want to come over for all the games? Will it streamline their devices and make life simpler? These are benefits.

In the case of job interviews the points on your resume and your experiences are features. They are not benefits. Nobody is really that interested. The only reason they are asking you questions about your resume and your experience is that they are trying to ascertain whether or not you are capable of solving their felt need.

They are trying to find the benefit of hiring you.

You should answer their questions! And you should clearly state all the features of you. Talk proudly about your resume and what you have learned from previous life experiences, but remember to tie the features to how the company benefits, better yet, how the interviewers benefit. Here is a helpful phrase to practice speaking in terms of benefits.

"...which means that you..."

In order to practice tying your features to their benefit add the phrase "which means that you..." to the end of each feature. Some examples would be:

"I received xyz award for customer satisfaction which means that you can rest assured that I know how to retain your hard earned customers."

"I have never been late to work which means that you can feel confident you're hiring a hard worker."

I have worked in a number of different industries which means that you don't have to worry about me having tunnel vision on your projects.

The benefits you state should have an emotional component to them. Once you are certain of their felt need, all of the benefits you speak of should target that felt need. For example, if you have uncovered that the interviewer fears too much time away from family because they have to stay late to fix the problems caused by their staff, you might say:

"I have a track record of timely and accurate reporting which means that you will spend more time with your family because you know my work is done correctly."

Fear & Greed

It has been said many times that all of sales comes down to fear and greed. You're either selling a solution that prevents people's fears or actualizes their greed (dreams). My experience tells me this is true and that fear is a more powerful motivator than even dreams. Insurance salesmen sell fear all the time. Politicians sell fear and greed.

When you are presenting the benefits the interviewers will receive by hiring you, it will almost always be targeting their fears or dreams which you have previously uncovered in the Discovery phase.

For each person there is one fear or one dream that overrides all other fears and dreams. That is the felt need. That is the "main thing."

Each interviewer has their own fears and dreams. So each may have a different felt need, a different "main thing," but each person only has one main thing. In the case of two interviewers you will have to identify each person's main thing and give benefits that answer each.

Chapter 17: The Right Attire

Regardless of whether you are getting ready for an interview or a new job, your appearance can enhance or hurt the impression you make. Clothes, combined with the right accessories make a visual statement. Though preferences change between organizations, there are some basic rules to follow. Keep in mind that some organizations still draw a distinct line between business and casual dress. For a good rule of thumb, pay a visit to the company before your interview to see how the people dress. Another way to make a statement is to dress a notch above the typical workday wear.

Women

Dress skirt and blouse

Pantyhose should be worn with dresses

Slip (make sure it's hidden!)

Business suits

Shoes: simple, low heels

Men

Suit and tie

Wear shoes that compliment the clothes. Typically, they should be dark in color.

Socks must be of the same color as your pants. Also, they should e high enough to ensure that your leg is not visible while you are sitting.

Sport coat and dress slacks

Other Tips:

Be conservative in your clothing. Trendy clothing with loud patterns and colors is considered unprofessional.

Do not wear loud colors or patterns and trendy clothing.

Overdressing is always better than under dressing.

Avoid strong cologne or perfume.

Wear simple jewellery and light make-up. Besides this, your accessories should compliment your outfit, not overshadow it.

Carry a briefcase with extra copies of application materials and a portfolio.

Hygiene is an important part of your overall personal. Therefore, ensure that you have trimmed nails and brushed teeth.

Before leaving, go to the bathroom and do a final check. Ensure that your hair is combed, skirt or tie is straightened, your shoes are clean, and hands are washed.

Chapter 18: What Would Your Boss/Professor Say About You?

This question is likely to come up in your interview. Nine times out of ten, the interviewer will contact your previous boss or professor in order to see what they have to say about you. It is not a smart idea to wait until the interview to "guess" what you think your boss/professor say about you.

What the Interviewer is looking for

According to Brian Krueger, founder of collegegrad.com, this question is a threat of reference. The interviewer wants to see if you are who you say you are, by getting the opinion of somebody who has seen you at work. They want to see how others perceive you; it is a true fact that other people perception is reality.

How to NOT Answer This Question

Don't answer this question by saying that you're not sure or you can't read minds. Demonstrating uncertainty will lead the interviewer to believe that you are unsure about your abilities and qualifications as a candidate.

How to Answer this Question

In order to answer this question as efficiently as possible, it is recommended that you talk to your previous or current professor/boss. Ask them, "What positive things can you say about me as far as a reference is concerned"? If they give you a positive response, ask for a letter of recommendation. If you can get a letter of recommendation, you'll be able to use their exact words as a response. Better yet, you can even provide the letter of recommendation during your interview (this shows that you are prepared). If you can't get a letter of recommendation on time, it's worthwhile to get a verbal reference and take some notes down.

Sample **Answer**

Q. What would your boss/professor say about you?

A. I believe my previous boss/professor would say that I'm Industrious, creative, consistent, flexible, and strategic. She/he would say this because he/she has seen me demonstrate these characteristics time and time again. In fact, I know she would say this because I have a recommendation letter in which she says so (this is a good time to ask the interviewer if you can show your letter of recommendation). She would add that if you have any questions about hiring me that you should give her a call.

This is a great answer because you are using the exact words from your boss/professor. Not only are you using their exact words, but you are also prepared to back it up with a physical letter of recommendation (this also shows the interviewer that you are prepared). The last part of this sample answer is a bit of a gutsy move, so say it with confidence, a smile and humor. The interviewer will appreciate your assertiveness.

Chapter 19: Types Of Interviews

There are different types of interview that you may be invited to attend in order for the company to get to know you and evaluate you as a person and check deeper the person mentioned on the hard copy of your resume. These types of interview are further broken down as below:

1.One on One interview: This is usually the most common way of interviewing for a job position from all the companies. Even if you are initially invited to participate on a different type of interview (as we will further mention them below), eventually the selected candidate or the final one or two candidates will proceed to a one on one interview. Usually on a one to one interview you should expect to meet the HR manager or the respective department manager of the position you have applied for. Sometimes the company may assign the interview to a key person of the same department as that person may be the project manager of the project you will be hired to work for. On such a kind of interview it is extremely important that you stay focused on the interviewer. If you lose your concentration and you start looking around the room while the interviewer is explaining you the key elements of the position then automatically you will lose your chance for the position. Pay close attention to what the interviewer is saying and make sure that you maintain a good eye contact until the interview is completed. A good eye contact demonstrates to the person that you are having the conversation with that they have your full attention and that you are highly interested on what they have to present and communicate over to you.

2.Panel Interviews: On a panel type of interview you should expect to meet multiple people at the same time such as the HR Manager, the respective department manager of the position your are applying for and in occasions a project manager of whom the duties of you work will fall under his / hers responsibilities and wings. When you attend this type of interview you should be very careful and imagine that every person attending the panel has an equal position of power within the company. You should again be careful with your eye contact. Maintain a good eye contact and look everyone briefly. Try to position your chair and body in such a way that you have a fair and equal viewing position of all members of the panel. At no point of the interview turn your back to any of the individuals of the panel. Also you should be careful not to give away all your attention and energy to a single person of the panel. If you notice that the questions are coming mostly from one person of the panel then when providing your answer make sure you provide equal eye contact to all participants.

3.Group Interviews: Group interviews are usually hosted from companies when they are evaluating multiple candidates at the same time providing different kind of tasks to the candidates to complete. Often they will gather all the candidates in one conference room and they will start group conversations by raising various topics. Through these tasks and group conversations the company assigned employees are trying to separate the best and more suitable candidate base on their behavior among the other candidates and towards them. On such type of interviews you should be able to demonstrate leadership in order to separate yourself but at the same time do not ask too many questions or dominate the conversation. Be polite to all around you as the company may include an employee of their own within the candidates in order to get a real and actual feedback on how you react under pressure to colleagues / candidates. At the same time and on the tasks assigned try to prove yourself when and as needed that you are a team player and that you can work great with other team members. At no point you should stay or remain too quiet as that will give the chance to the candidates to promote their selves. Stay alert and be sure to follow up on the conversations and tasks as needed.

4.Video Conference Interviews: Video conference interviews are usually arranged when a candidate is geographically located on a different city / state or country from the actual location of the company. A video interview will provide the chance to the company to get to know you and conclude if they would like to proceed or not to a second interview with you as a candidate without have to worry that if they go ahead and invite you to a one to one interview due to the allocation costs that they will feel committed to hire you as well. This type of interview is taking place by the use of communication computer software such as Skype or Lync according to availability. The candidate will be asked to establish or accept a video call invitation from the company where the company will be able to see and hear the candidate via a web camera and a microphone. When scheduled for a video conference interview you should make sure and test beforehand that all your necessary equipment such as web camera, headset and microphone are working successfully. You should then allocate a specific location in your house or office that you will establish this video interview. When deciding on which will be the most appropriate area to choose be mindful of the background that your interviewer will be able to see. Make sure that there is enough brightness and light and that this will be facing you and not located behind you. If the source of light is in front of you then the interviewer will be able to see your face clearly while if the source of light is exactly behind you the interviewer will be able to see a dark shadowed face. Before the actual interview you should practice in front of a web camera in order to become more familiar with the process and be more relaxed on the actual interview itself without worrying how you may sound or look like. Make sure that you sit straight and that you keep your answers short and your voice is clear. This demonstrates confidence.

5.Telephone Interviews: Telephone interviews is another way of the company to have a first meeting experience with the candidate when a one to one interview is not feasible due to geographic location and long distances or when Video conference option is not available due to lack of technology or equipment. When scheduled for a telephone interview you should make sure that you have a

notepad in front of you to keep notes. It is proven that when people are hosting phone conferences are easier to forget some points and details mentioned during the call. If you are going to use a cell phone or a mobile device to participate then you make sure that the device that you will be using is fully charged and will be able to last long enough for the duration of the interview. Choose a quiet place that there is no background noise so that you can focus easily on the interviewer. Once the phone call is in place provide enough time and make sure that the interviewer has completed asking the question before start answering. When you are talking or answering smile! Smiling is something that is noticeable even through phone conversations and it demonstrates enthusiasm and approachability. There is no coincidence that they say a smile goes a long way.

6.Dining / Lunch Interviews: Usually this type of interview is conducted within smaller size of companies or when a candidate is suggested for a job position from an already existing employee, a friend or a family member. The manager / owner and director of the company is in most of the cases the person who will do the interview and due to heavy schedule arranges the interview over lunch or dinner. Other reason may be that that manager of the company would like to host the interview process in a more comfortable environment where the candidate gets to be more of himself /

herself. When you are scheduled for such a type of interview do not forget that is still a job interview. Do not attend the meeting and be too casual. When you are asked to order your food keep it simple. Do not order anything too expensive and nothing that is too messy. Avoid ordering any alcohol and mind your manners at all times.

Chapter 20: Sample Resume

Name: Your name with initial (Do not furnish @Alias name)
Address: Your present address for communication
Contact No.: Your cell no /landline no
E-mail: Your mail ID (Avoid obscene and objectionable words in ID) **Photograph**: optional, file size gets bigger for embedded images

Career Summary

Develop it as a short paragraph of approximately 50-60 words in third person singular. Write about your career aspirations and what you have to offer to the market.

Include your skills, attitude, knowledge and work experience. See that it is supported in the CV content.

No hypes, jargons and mockery words

Key Skills

Develop this section in the bulleted format, to make your CV reader friendly.

Write about the key skills you have gained during your last employments. Focus on the skills relevant to the position you are applying to.

List out any special, out of work activity that could support your personality.

You can mention some of your key responsibility areas.

Work Experience

Write this section of your CV in chronologically descending order

Designation, company name followed by duration of work. For example: **Marketing Manager, XYZ company, April 2000 to Oct 2001**

Brief on Job responsibilities below the position details in bullets. Do not copy and paste the entire JD.

Never try to fill up a gap between jobs with fake data or with anything that would please a recruiter /interviewer.

Achievements

Write this section also in a bulleted format on rank of priority

It should tell the prospective employer, "This is what I did for my last employer, I can do it for you also."

Do not try to copy your colleague's data as yours. Speak truth. If there is nothing to mention, leave it. It is not compulsory.

If fresher, you mention the prizes won/certificates received.

Never mention with pride if you had participated in public agitations and had been sentenced.

Educational Qualification

Write this section of your CV also in bullets

For a role, if your qualification is higher than what is actually expected, do not focus your CV on the qualifications. (So customise CV for different positions that will suit you. Do not mix up resumes and send the recruiter. You are likely to turn up for interview with a wrong one.)

Interests

Write about other interests, languages known, hobby in bullets

Personal Details

Father's /Husband's Name

Date of Birth
Languages Known
Marital status

Date /Place Signature

A fresher resume should be simple and all subheadings need not be copied from an experienced CV. A fresher need not carry the usual 'Objective' stating 'I would like to work in a challenging role that would utilise my skill and work experience.' The goal is to seek employment and get trained. If so, how did he gain experience previously? What if it does not turn out to be challenging? So, try to be truly genuine and original without hype.

'Voice Resume' as audio file is becoming popular. This way they get to know the candidate's capabilities. [An employer does not know who scripted and lent the voice. It will be exposed in a live interview.]

Many candidates are transforming the CV into a Declaration Form. As said, a Résumé is only a summary and there is nothing you have to declare on assets or liabilities as expected on government papers.

CV is neither a statement of confession nor a WILL / AGREEMENT to declare your statement. Unless specifically mentioned or demanded to include in print, do not state 'I declare that the information given above is true to the best of my knowledge and belief.'

(If so, who prepared your CV without your knowledge and belief? You prepared it with document evidence viz degree certificate, experience letters etc. The documents are physically available with you in hard copy that can be called for verification at the time of job offer.)

Chapter 21: Non-Verbal Communication

So much of an interview is based on non-verbal communication and that includes your body language. In this chapter will discuss a few skills that fall under non-verbal communication that can show the interviewer that you are the perfect candidate for the job by just using your body.

Posture: posture equals presence, make sure you work on your posture before you enter an interview, most of us are used to placing our hands on the desk and laying on them, that is wrong make sure you work on your body posture that is your shoulders back, head up posture. Standing up or sitting up gives confidence, it shows your professionalism in a non-verbal communicative way.

Eye Contact: you have to make eye contact in an interview, a lot of time when people are nervous, they tend to look up and may be look away as they tell their story. This gives an indication to the interviewer that you are unsure and not confident, because by so doing you find that you are not giving a good representation of yourself and your capabilities. Making and maintaining eye contact shows focus in what you are doing and whom you are talking to because they are what matters at that particular moment, it also shows that confidence towards the position. You can always practice that when you are out there with people going about your day today business by making eye contact and not look around everytime you are talking to them. I know some people are naturally nervous but it is important if you train yourself to always make and maintain eye contact.

Lean Forward to Engage: so far you been sitting up straight and making eye contact showing the assured, confidence in you and in the job, but how do you show them non-verbally your interest in the job, by leaning in.

How to Respond to Interview Questions: At this point, applying good listening skill is very important. Listen to the questions attentively, avoid talking when your interviewer is talking, ask for a repeat if you didn't get the question and give a correct and precise response. Avoid digressions or repetitions when answering questions, answer in time, and be sure of your response for this is your opportunity to impress your interviewers with your answers.

Dress Code: Your dress code to an interview is as important as preparing yourself for interview questions and answers. Your appearance makes the first impression about you to your interviewer, so you should dress responsibly avoiding clothing that is too tight, exposes your body parts or offensive combination of colors. Dress code is essential for acquiring a professional position.

Always Wear a Confident Smile: A confident smile is considered an essential and necessary tip as far as the interview is concerned. When you know what you want, go for it with sure as a smile is inevitable as "Your smile is your Logo."

The Basics of Body Language for a Perfect Interview

First, let's look into why body language is so important in interviews. First, body language is important because the employer will be reading your nonverbal cues. They will be listening to your words, but they will also be looking at how you are acting. Body language is something that everyone notices, so this is also true about your interviewer. They will notice if you are not making eye contact, and they will assume this is because you are nervous or not confident. They will also notice if you have a firm handshake, and they will believe you are confident and that you are successful through this. Because the interviewer is going to be noticing your body language, you should be noticing your own as well. If you are aware of your own body language, you can control it.

Let's talk about power body language. Power body language is a way to use your nonverbal communication to seem successful and confident. If you use body language that makes you appear confident, it will give you power in situations like interviews. Let's look into the components of power body language and the other body language tools you should use when you are in an interview.

First, make sure that you have a strong handshake. A strong handshake shows you are confident and successful. It shows you are not afraid of what is going to happen.

Shake the interviewer's hand with a firm hand and a strong shake.

While you are shaking the interviewer's hand, introduce yourself, and make eye contact. Eye contact is important in your handshake, but it is also important for the rest of the interview at the same time. Eye contact is important because it shows you are both confident and interested. If you do not make eye contact, it can make you either seem like you are not interested in the job or it can make you seem like you are nervous. Both of these qualities are things that they are definitely not interested in. If you make eye contact, however, you seem interested and confident. These are qualities that people who are conducting interviews will see, and they will want. Eye contact is an easy thing to do, so it is something that you should always include in your interview skills.

You should also make sure that you are smiling. If you are smiling, it shows you were happy to be there. It shows you are friendly and that you are interested in the job. It shows you were happy to have the chance to interview for the job that you are seeking. It shows you are confident and you deserve to be there. It shows you are good enough and you believe it. If it might seem like you are not interested in the job or that you feel you do not deserve to be there. You do not want this to be the case, so make sure you keep a smile on your face.

Also, make sure that your body language is relaxed. Try to relax your jaw as this helps you relax the rest of your body. If you are relaxed, you will seem more confident and less nervous. Most employers want laid-back employees and not stressed ones. For this, if you seem relaxed, you will see more like the type of employee that they are looking for.

Make sure that you also sit and stand with your shoulders back. Sit up straight and keep the appropriate amount of distance in between you and then if you are. If you do this, you will seem like you are confident and that you are respectful towards the person interviewing you.

Other tools that can be helpful include active listening. Active listening includes eye-contact, nodding your head, smiling and letting the interviewer speak. It means you will never interrupt the interview while they are speaking. Typically, interviews are always about the applicant. This can be tiring for the person who is conducting the interview. If you show you are interested in what the interviewer says and that you care about them as a person, you can help them to feel better, and your interview in the process. The person who is conducting your interview is likely to remember this feeling.

Your body language can help you show you are interested in the job. Consider bringing a notebook and pen with you and taking notes on what you are saying. Also, you could include in this notebook a list of questions. When the interviewer gives you the answers to these questions, you could write the answers down in your notebook.

This shows you are serious, and it shows you are prepared. It shows you care enough about the job to bring notes home to read later. This is also a step that most people do not take the time or effort to do. For this, it can make you stand out from the crowd. I can make the interviewer remember you long after the interview has taken place.

As you can see, there are many things to remember when you are in an interview. When you get to an interview, the person who is interviewing you liked your application so much that they wanted to meet you in person. This will likely give you a boost of confidence because you already know that you were set apart in a small group of successful applicants. It means your application was considered better than many others. Interviews can be nerve-racking but think of them as a way to make a great first impression. You already made a great first impression on paper; you just need to do it in person now.

Chapter 22: Top Job Interview Questions

In one word, describe yourself.

When you get to this kind of question, you have to understand what the interviewer is trying to do: get inside your head. Hiring is a gamble. Companies always worry about who they're hiring. The person that hires you also has an interest in how well you go because they can be blamed if you aren't a good hire.

So you'll want to refer to the four basic questions to help inform your answer: Are you capable of doing the job? Do you have an understanding of the job? Will you be able to do the job? Do you pose a risk to this person's continued employment?

If you don't do well in this position, you'll find yourself posing quite a huge risk to another person. So in order to get an idea of how well you will do, they ask some odd questions like this one.

There are a lot of words to pick from. There's dynamic, motivated, successful, responsible, strategic, dedicated, creative, flexible, reliable, dependable, fair, helpful, valuable, enthusiastic, organized, steady, focused, honest, and many more words that you could use to describe yourself. This is a really hard question to pin down.

Personally, I use 'dynamic.' This word works because I'm adaptive and do whatever is necessary to succeed. It's an all-purpose word that applies to many different jobs. However, I want you to avoid just picking a word for yourself. You'll need to think about your job and the kind of words that might fit well with this job.

Every answer that you give is hopefully leading you to a job offer. So you will need to be aware at every point. Don't think about this question as just about who you and what you are like, but focus on how you can relate that back to the job. You might pick a trait that will help you stand out from the rest of the applicants. You might want to use 'bright' because you're quite smart, but 'successful' will probably be a better fit for the employer.

Other good words include responsible, dependable, creative, flexible, strategic, dedicated, motivated, valuable, enthusiastic, organized, steady, focused, honest, fair, helpful, and reliable. Regardless of what you want to pick, think about the job and what kinds of traits are good for someone in this particular position. Be aware that this question can also be followed by a request for an explanation or example that shows off this trait, so you'll want to be prepared with at least one story that can show off the word that you have chosen.

Do you like working alone or with a time?

This question is fairly common, but that doesn't mean that it isn't a tricky one to deal with. While they are asking about your preference, there are few jobs that you will find that don't have you working both in a team and alone at some point. That's where the tricky nature of this question comes into play. You might actually prefer one, but saying so will cause you more problems. Being comfortable with both work styles is really important for many jobs.

There are some standard answers, such as, "I work well both ways. I do great when I work as a team, but I'm also comfortable when working alone." However, you'll really want to see if you can improve this answer. In order to improve it, you will need to know a little bit about the job that you are trying to get into. You'll need to know what is typically part of the job. This might be research that you complete ahead of the interview or things that you might know from working similar jobs.

So after looking at the job, you might be able to use an answer like, "I typically prefer working alone; however, working with a team can help creatively because we can bounce ideas around and it helps us learn from each other" or "I usually prefer to work in a group, but having a part of a project that is my own is also nice at times."

Both of these answers get at your preference without being outright negative about the other side of the situation. This positivity is extremely important. A hiring manager will feel much more confident hiring someone that is confident and positive. Flexibility is a desirable attribute in people.

However, we suggest that you don't just stop at answering the question. Ask them a question back about the situation like, "Roughly how much time is spent working with a time versus time I will spend working on my own?" You can ask about the kind of environment that the business encourages. This allows you to not only learn more about the situation but also keeps the conversation going.

Have you had to conform to a policy that you did not agree with? Tell me about that time.

We have discussed behavioral interview questions already. The key to the answer is usually the STAR (situation or task, action, result) structure for the story, but this question is one that you don't want to have a good story about. This question is possibly worse than asking you about a difficult situation that you handled. This one prevents you from looking like you overcame something. Instead, it's showing you in possibly one of your lowest moments. You're not going to look good during this question.

You'll want to think carefully about your answer to this kind of question. What made you not conform at first with the policy? What made you conform in the end? You may think of yourself as some sort of martyr in the situation, but someone else might not see that. In fact, if the policy was bad enough, you might come out looking pretty bad.

You might have known something that your previous boss didn't know, but that doesn't make you look good either. That's getting close to badmouthing your former employer. That's something you should definitely avoid. In fact, that kind of answer might get you in trouble with your new boss or even prevent you from getting into this new job.

When you get to the heart of the matter, most people can't really affect the policies at their work. All of those rules are set up by someone else and you can't do much to influence them. Even if you bring information to the table, you might not be able to change anything or get a message across. If you don't comply, you could lose your job.

With this answer, you'll have to be careful. This question is hard, but it's also giving the potential employer a lot of good information. They're wanting to know how you communicated, whether or not you confronted your boss, and if you managed to avoid the situation entirely.

The best answer might simply be, "Sorry, I can't recall that happening in my previous jobs." Of course, this might not be enough to stop the interviewer. If they press, you can follow up with, "If this happened, I would probably ask questions or express my concern. It is part of my job to support the rest of the team. That included bringing potential issues into the light so they can be dealt with before they actually become problems. However, the decision belongs to my supervisor in the end." You are showing that you think critically, work with the team, and respect authority. This kind of answer can be really attractive to potential employers.

Describe a time where you believe you went beyond the call of duty.

This is the best kind of question to get. It's a behavioral interview question, but this kind of question really gives you a chance to shine. This is the kind of story that you should always have on hand. Exceeding expectations is always a good thing to talk about. This shows that you bring quite a bit of value when you work.

You should always have a story prepared before you go into the interview. Try to pick one that will speak to the job that you are applying for, not just the job that you have had in the past. Speaking of what you can offer in the future is always a good choice. You can focus on particular skills or tasks that might be in your future with this job. The situation should be a little bit difficult. Conflict and resolution are always part of a good narrative.

The general story should follow this outline, "We needed (blank) done. There were some specific tasks that we needed to do. I did X, Y, and Z. These were the results of the situation."

This is just following the STAR method. It will really help you get the most out of your story. Don't feel like you have to hold back or not brag. This is a situation where you are meant to brag. This will help you show off your best qualities and also show you communicate well. You can even provide a 'brag book' which will be a physical representation of what you did and show all of the proof of what you did. Combine a good story with the book and you'll have major points in this interview.

If you were made to choose to become any animal in the planet, what would your choice be, and why would you pick it?

While a job interview tends to be a formal affair, there are some interviewers who are fond of throwing the prospective applicants a few curveballs. Their reasoning behind this can vary. Some think that your answer to such an odd question would reveal much about you. Others may just want to find out your reaction when confronted with an unexpected situation, like being asked such a question out of the blue. Whatever reason the interviewer has for asking, these questions do offer a hint into how you think, and these questions can be seen as opportunities to display your wit and quick thinking. After all, when you head into an interview, you should be prepared for anything they may throw your way. One of the better methods to get in the right mindset for an interview is to think about what qualities and attributes are most suited to the job you're seeking. If you're able to identify this, you'll have a much easier time answering any type of question appropriately. You can use this insight to prepare answers on how who you are as a person, your personality, your skills, or even your hobbies make you well-suited for the job.

For this specific type of question, picking a specific animal isn't really important, but rather, making sure that you can link your choice and the attributes needed for the job is. Of course, it would be best to avoid picking animals that already have negative attributes associated with them, like bugs, snakes, or even chickens. Once you've made your choice, you have to start explaining the reasoning behind it. You should link yourself to the animal, explaining the similarities that you find. Some examples would be liking yourself to an eagle, at least if you're going for a higher position, but that comparison may be unfavorable for jobs that need lots of cooperation. Horses are also a good choice, as they are strong and hard workers, who function just as well solo or as part of a bigger group. Ants are diligent and known as tenacious and hard workers, as well as being one of the best team players in the animal kingdom. Dogs are known for their loyalty and friendliness, which may suit certain roles. Many other animals may prove to be good choices to display your chosen attributes, just make sure you are able to link them properly. If the interview is going well, you may even be able to end it on a light note by asking your interviewer what he would choose if the question was posed to him.

If you could rewind the clock, repeating the last ten years, how would you choose to do things?

This is a question that invites much thought. After all, we tend to have many regrets, big and small. We may regret speeding that one time on a country road, investing in a bad portfolio, buying a bad outfit, or any number of other things we wish we didn't do. However, when it comes to this question being posed during an interview, the interviewer is most likely thinking of something else. This question is in fact designed to make you reveal what you feel your weaknesses are. This question tends to draw out your flaws, as they can see that based on what you regret. This question may be a good opportunity to address any possible issues you had in your past work history, and in fact, this question may be triggered by their knowledge of such issues. For example, if they see that you have had a previous employment that lasted for a suspiciously short time before you left, this may pique their interest enough to ask the question. You can explain this in a diplomatic manner, perhaps saying that you regret quitting your job to take another, saying that it didn't turn out to be a good move, but when it happened, it was the best decision you felt you could make with the information you had available. You can follow that up saying that regardless, you learned much from it, but if you knew what would happen, you wouldn't have done it. Try to frame issues as positively as you can, but do not lie. If you lie, you're out of the running for sure.

If your career has been on the smooth side, and there are no incidents to really explain, then you may be able to answer this with a lighter note. If you want to be more serious when answering however, you can say that while everyone has regrets, decisions and choices that they wish they could reverse, you are happy with the general direction and trajectory of your life, both career-wise and personal. That answer is fairly neutral, while showing the interviewer that you have not really made any major mistakes that you truly wish you could reverse, and that answer will most likely do its job in most situations.

Do you consider yourself more concerned with the overall scheme of things, or with the smaller details, the nitty-gritty?

This question is obviously asking how you tend to work. The answer depends on the person, but in truth, the question is complicated. Though your interviewer is only asking you to choose one option, all employers would like their employees to be both kinds. If a person tends to work with the bigger picture in mind, they also want to make sure they know how to deal with the smaller details. If a person focuses on the smaller things, employers also want to make sure that they are aware of the bigger goal, and that their employees avoid getting tunnel vision.

The best answer is one that implies that you are both. You can choose one, but include a statement that shows that you are not exclusively that type of person. For example, if you are an accountant, you are most likely to be one that focuses on the little details, however, saying that you also know how to step back and look at things from a distance would help show that you are well-rounded. If you are interviewing for a higher position, especially one more concerned with strategy, then saying that while you tend to look at the strategic goals, you also do not lose sight of the smaller things that need to be dealt with in order to get there.

Chapter 23: Ways To Hugely Boost Your Job Interview Success Rate

So often, a job interviewer is faced with several candidates who, according to their resume, have similar experiences. Not until you reach the interview stage will they be able to judge the candidate's personality. But this too may result in several very identical candidates with little to distinguish between them.

So how do you stand out from the crowd? If you can offer something unique, then you have a much better chance of success. You just cannot be ignored.

What could be unique about your application? It doesn't have to be the fact that you are the best at something, although this would help. It just means you need to offer something that the other candidates cannot provide or forget to highlight; it's the same thing.

So in what areas can you stand up and say 'I have a unique selling point?'

For all job interviews, the interviewer has a recurring question in their heads..... What is the problem I need the candidate to solve? This is a good starting place. Most candidates will never indeed find this out. They do not ask or understand its importance. You must try to find this out. You can then tailor your skills and experience to demonstrate how you can address this issue. Here is an example:

Job: 'We are looking to employ a salesman so that we can increase turnover.

Actual problem: 'We need to increase turnover because we struggle to make any profits. Every time we make a sale, we hardly make any profit because our sales channel is very inefficient'.

Candidate: 'I see. We had the same problem at my last company. What we did was introduce several new methods of selling. We set up an e-commerce website, grew our joint venture sales partnerships, and brought our inflated advertising budget in house. All three initiatives meant that sales increased by 35%, but the cost base actually stayed neutral. The gross profit figure, therefore, rose by 74%. I was instrumental in driving through these changes. It sounds like you have a similar situation to ours 15 months ago, which I am sure I can assist you with. Do you want to hear more about how I did this?'

YES, of course, he does!

You have a unique selling point. You have faced this situation before and can directly relate your experience to the task at hand. The job interviewer must be impressed with such a reply. They already imagine the success you can bring to the job role. How on earth could anybody fail to be impressed?

The unique selling point does not have to be hidden. You may be an exceptional candidate because you are the only candidate who actually convinces the interviewer that you meet the job description.

This is where preparation is so necessary. List the details of the job description and make sure you have prepared answers with relevant examples that demonstrate you can meet all these criteria. By default, this may cause you unique.

How else can you make yourself unique?

If you have a particular skill which you know is in short supply, eg. "I have used software x for 18 months. I am quite proud of my achievements in mastering it because I was reading recently that very few people have this skill, and there is a long learning curve.'

It plants the seed of doubt in the interviewers' mind that the other candidates without these skills might take a long time to learn this. In contrast, I have a candidate in front of me who has already learned this and can start being productive almost immediately.

Be careful, though, not to directly criticize other candidates either directly or indirectly.

Look through your resume and find examples of what may be rare or unique.

'Do you have experience of selling a particular product range?'

'Have you led large teams of staff?'

'Do you have a particular qualification that other candidates might not have?'

'Have you experience public speaking.'

Your unique selling point may not necessarily need to be a tangible skill, qualification, or experience. It could be that you are the most determined candidate, the most enthusiastic candidate, or the most likely to fit into a team environment.

Note down the things that you excel at using these to form a list of strengths. You may then need to whittle this list down again to identify those traits that you believe to be unique. Of course, you cannot know for sure, but by concentrating on these, your chances of success will undoubtedly be enhanced.

Get the interviewer to say 'yes' in their mind. Control the flow of positive information. An interviewer needs to see you in a positive light. One of the ways to do this is to get them to say 'yes' in their minds.

The most effective way of doing this is to control the level of positive information they are receiving. An interviewer will review your resume and begin with the premise that you are 'on paper' suitably qualified to fulfill the role.

They will start the interview with 'Let us review your last few roles and tell me what you did (and achieved)?'

This allows you to detail all the positive elements of your career. List the benefits you have brought to the role. This is fine, but the other candidates will get the same treatment!

However, to separate the candidates, the interviewer will undoubtedly delve into the negative aspects of what you have done.

'Tell me a time when you fell short or didn't achieve your goals'

'What aspects of your last job did you not like?'

'Why have you got gaps in your resume?'

The list of negative questions that an interviewer can ask are almost endless and are always the toughest questions to handle.

An interviewer will often discount the positive aspects of your answers and look much more closely at the potential negatives in your career. You should not be afraid to discuss the negative aspects of your career. A successful series of answers will put you in a strong position. It clears a lot of uncertainty in the interviewers' minds.

The key point is to keep any negative answers or information to a minimum and accentuate the positives.

Here are examples of what not to say:

Q. 'Have you ever disagreed or argued with your current immediate supervisor?'

A. 'Sometimes when we disagree on certain aspects of my work.'

Q. 'Presumably, you want this job because you are disillusioned with your current employer?'

A. 'Yes, and the pay isn't great, either'.

Q. 'You seem to lack experience in area 'x.'

A. 'Yes, I never got the opportunity to train in it.'

If you answered like this, then you are just re-enforcing the negative aspects of the question. You must never answer negative questions in this manner. If you do, then you can say goodbye to any job offers.

Look at the following examples and see how a negative question is snuffed out and turned into a positive.

Q. 'Have you ever disagreed or argued with your current immediate supervisor?'

A. 'Fortunately, we have always had a good working relationship. Recently he has been giving me higher powers of authority, and also I have been trusted to delegate for him and weekly performance meetings.'

Nip the negative in the bud and then accentuate the positive by detailing the fact that your supervisor is comfortable with giving you more powers of the trust.

Q. 'Presumably, you want this job because you are disillusioned with your current employer?'

A. 'Actually. I have enjoyed working for my current employer, and they have given me plenty of valuable experience. However, I now feel it is time to further my career by moving on and learning new skills.'

Notice how you start the sentence with the word 'actually,' or fortunately, this is better than saying an outright 'NO.'

It may appear only a minor point, but don't start the sentence with 'No, on the contrary......' or words to that effect. It effectively disagrees with the interviewer, and this is bad diction.

Q. 'You seem to lack experience in using this type of software.'

A. 'This may be true, but I have used very similar software at my current organization, which I learned to use very quickly and became proficient at using in a short period.

You need to accept there is a shortcoming. But the approach is to close off the objection by showing how it shouldn't be a problem for the employer and try not to discuss it any further.

Q. 'Describe a situation where your work was criticized.'

This is a tricky question because it has got 'expand on some negative aspects of your work' written all over it. Firstly do not say that your work has never been criticized. It just sounds too unlikely.

Change the question around so that it is not your work that was criticized but an idea you had. Ideas are often considered, criticized, then dropped with little or no impact on the organization. Bad work will result in pain for the organization.

A good answer is to refer to a team meeting where you were all asked to contribute ideas and not necessarily in an area with which you were familiar. Say you suggested something, but upon discussion, it was felt there were some flaws in the idea, and a better approach was adopted.

Add a humbling statement such as ' in our work all team members are often encouraged to contribute ideas and provide honest criticism on each other's ideas. No one in the group takes criticism personally as the objective of the exercise is to explore all possibilities, eliminate the poor suggestions, and find the best solution.'

Such an answer accepts that you are not perfect but implies the criticism of your idea ended in a positive outcome.

Do not criticize other people or ex-employers. Continuing with the theme of removing all negative thoughts from the interview, do not criticize your past employer or employees. This is not a forum for letting off steam and ranting on about an ex-employer or employee. Interviewers are prospective employees and do not want to hear anything negative from you. Criticizing ex-employers or ex-employees could lose you the job there and then.

People do not like whiners, however much it may be justified. Mentioning this and raises the question in their mind that you may have been partly to blame for any antipathy.

It immediately raises the question - are you the trouble maker? Is it you that cannot get on with people?

Ask yourself a straightforward question.

In what way can be bad-mouthing an ex-employee help in furthering your interview and get you the job?

The answer is absolutely nothing.

If you didn't get on with someone, which, after all, is fairly common, avoids mentioning it. If, in the unlikely event, you are asked about any difficulties with ex-employees or your working relationship, deny any friction existed. Keep it general, and do not talk about any person or position specifically.

"I always endeavor to maintain a positive and professional working relationship with all colleagues. I am a great believer in the team ethic and getting along with colleagues, as I believe this is the most effective and productive approach."

To remind you if you are talking about anything apart from you, then you are losing valuable 'bragging time' to shine.

Do not argue or disagree with the interviewer.

It is simple. If you argue or disagree with the interviewer, you will undoubtedly fall in their estimations. What is more, if by arguing or disagreeing with them, they do not like you, your chances of success are reduced to between very low and zero.

To summarise, keep all negatives aspects of the interview to a minimum. The aim is to get the interviewer to nod their head and say 'YES subconsciously'.

Don't be overbearing or overpowering, show the interviewer up or threaten their job. When it comes to showing you are confident and self-assured, there is a level at which you need to pitch this. On the one extreme, there is the nervous, unconfident, and desperate-sounding individual. At the other height, there is the overbearing, arrogant, boastful individual.

It is not uncommon to hear of interviewers citing examples of individuals who come for an interview professing to be able to rewrite the company rule book and 'sort things out' for the good of the company.

Maybe they can, and perhaps they do have the best interests of their prospective employers' at heart.

However, if the poor interviewer thinks this person is going to show them up as being weak or even threaten their job, then they will not get the job. It is as simple as that. You would never employ someone who could potentially ruin your career. They are looking for someone who is ideally going to enhance the work they do and make them look good.

Everyone is conscious that they have failings. A manager does not want to take on anyone who may expose their weaknesses or make apparent the current flaws they may have in their role.

Don't be modest, Throughout this book, we have emphasized the need to show the prospective employer that you have the necessary attributes to do the job and bring additional benefits to the role. This takes a certain degree of boasting.

We are brought up to believe that we need to be modest to fit in with the crowd. Well, modesty is exceptional in an interview as long as it doesn't get in the way of expressing your attributes and skills to the full.

You need to express your career and work achievements in specific terms with relevant examples. Additionally, you need to show your soft skills and attributes again with appropriate standards.

It is essential to write these down and practice them. Make them sound real.

It is fairly non-specific and also smacks of boasting. No one likes to hear someone needlessly boasting. Anyway, you mentioned your ex-boss, does this mean you have already left the company, and you are now unemployed, or are you so sure of getting this job?

It is essential to get the wording right and so write down each statement and practice it. Have at least three achievements you can quite for each stage of your career. Practice them so that they sound natural and are not boastful.

You need to avoid meaningless phrases like 'I work hard' and 'I am very efficient at my job,' 'I am a good salesman.'

A prospective employer is looking for a sharp individual who can communicate precisely and effectively. The above phrases are woolly non-descript and convey little specific meaning. The interviewer then has to probe deeper.

'What makes you a good salesman, what were your sales figures for the last six months?'

Your first question allowed you to list your main strengths. If ever there was a question with which you needed to practice a full and detailed answer, which contains your strengths and abilities, then this is it. So having asked the question once, if you do not provide the benefits, the interviewer effectively needs to ask the same question again. So be full and specific in your answers. Avoid meaningless phrases. The interview is the one opportunity for you to shine!

Always tell the truth (be careful about exaggerating).

When asked a direct question, always tell the truth. If you are caught contradicting yourself, then you can wave goodbye to the job.

Of course, if there is something you don't want to discuss, then don't bring it up. Do not offer negative information. It is up to the interviewer to get the 'dirty facts.' It is up to you to paint the rosiest picture possible.

Exaggeration is a grey area in interview techniques. Most people will try to embellish their skills, ability, and importance to the organization.

Studies have shown that it is more important how you say something than what you say. Also, the English language allows so much scope for delivering the same facts in several different ways.

That is why preparation is the key to success not only in what you say but how you present those words and how you present yourself. The facts of what you say become less critical in interviews.

So the bottom line is there is no need to exaggerate. Although it may be tempting to do so, it is easier to be successful by effectively delivering your skills and ability.

Just keep smiling

Some sure interviewers know little or nothing about interviewing. Maybe they are nervous or just not properly trained. We have all seen interviewers who seem to trot out question after question without seemingly listening to your answer. They may not even look up at you or acknowledge your answer with a smile or a nod of the head.

It can be so frustrating in these situations. You are trying to build rapport, but you seem to face a brick wall. Don't worry! Just keep persevering. All the candidates are likely to face the same response. Do not take this personally. You need to view this as an opportunity. Other candidates may well look at this 'hostility' as a sign they are performing poorly and give up.

This book prepares you for an interview to project yourself in the best light. The fact that you are struggling to build any rapport with the interviewer, while in itself, is disconcerting, does not mean you are necessarily saying the wrong things or projecting the false image.

An interview will typically last one hour, so make sure you stay the distance and do not get disheartened. Keep smiling!

The one drawback with an interviewer like this is that it does give you a wrong impression of the company. After all, you are probably going to have to work with this individual. Once you are offered the job, you can always turn it down if there is something you didn't like.

Chapter 24: Preparing For Role-Plays And Last-Minute Tips Before You Go

There are little words that serve to strike fear in the hearts of candidates all over the world. Role Play Interview. Might be tough to train for, difficult to conduct and deeply overwhelming, the task of performing this activity can be daunting even for a seasoned professional.

But don't fret. With an appreciation of the intent of the role plays, in addition to the structure for you to plan and use on a day, it is more than likely to do well. Here are some tips to help you tap on the right boxes.

What's the purpose of a role play interview?

A role-play is a virtual representation of a real-life scenario. When this test is used in an interview, the goal is to put the applicant in a position that is close to the usual circumstances of the work and to see how they respond.

Role plays are commonly used in recruiting, particularly for clients facing or people performing positions. The investigator may usually take on the role of customer or contractor, and the applicant will be asked to complete the assignment, here are some examples.

This could be to market a particular product, resolve a dispute, or mentor a member of the team. The basic principle is that the applicant should effectively complete the mission to the best of his abilities.

How am I supposed to prepare for the role play?

It is important that you prepare for your role long before you receive a brief on the day of your interview. Next, identify the expertise and talents that the interviewer is likely to be looking for you to show.

For a selling or customer service job, they will be looking for you to demonstrate the ability to ask big questions, to respond appropriately, to address challenges and to close the deal at the appropriate time.

You're going to need evidence of excellent communication and reasoning skills. Fill out our Customer Service Roles Planning sheet for more information on what interviewers are asking for.

For a people management role, they will be looking for you to listen and show sympathy and expect to see your coaching and motivational abilities. Practice using a coaching model like GROW to frame your questions.

If you're applying for a sales job, you're likely to need to sell a product when playing a role. To guide you through the process, consider learning about and using the 7-step method to form the dialogue.

If you're applying for a customer service role, you're likely to need to resolve a complaint. Often, it is helpful to have a structure to help you through the scenario, such as this one.

The day you are handed a brief on the day of the interview, your greatest asset will be your ability to manage your time of preparation. Read the summary carefully, at least twice, looking for clues as to what the interviewer could anticipate.

Remember the details of the case—what, specifically, is the intended outcome they are aiming for? What are the challenges you're likely to face? Reflect on similar situations that you may have been struggling with in the past—what went well? What didn't happen?

Most essential of all, try to relax. Take a deep breath and clear your mind. Write down any questions you'd like to pose during the role play. Ask how you're going to deal with unforeseen opposition. And always keep an eye on the result.

With the correct planning, there's no need to think about a role play question. Note, the interviewer is not trying to catch you—

the object of the exercise is to give you the opportunity to show your skills and abilities. Through following our advice, you'll feel prepared and positive about the day.

Role-Plays:

Let's get going. So, what's a role-play exercise?

A role-play exercise is an assessment activity in which candidates act on an imaginary scenario that closely reflects a situation that could occur in the job they have applied for.

What happens during a role-playing exercise? Role-play games are in a fairly standard format:

1) You must provide a summary sheet that describes the situation and goals and will be given 20-30 minutes to prepare.

2) Then you continue the role-play. Usually with one of the assessors–it will often be the line manager for one of the positions being recruited.

3) At the conclusion of the test, you will be assessed on your quality and suggestions will be taken into account in the overall outcomes of the interview or assessment centre.

Clearly, the scope of your role-play brief varies depending on your business, but the basic framework of the role-plays appears to stay the same.

What do employers want to see in a role-play exercise?

Role-Play Interview Performance An interview or appraisal center role-play can be an exhilarating experience, but these' company games' are an important part of almost any major employer recruitment process. Let's take a look at how to succeed in your role-play.

A role-play exercise is an assessment activity in which candidates act on an imaginary scenario that closely reflects a situation that could occur in the job they have applied for.

What do managers want to see in a role-play exercise?

To offer you a better idea of what to expect, let's look at 2 real-world examples. Here are two simple examples of briefs often used by large corporate recruiters:

Reference role-play practice

Angry Customer

"You are the sales manager of a small company. You receive a phone call from an angry customer who has bought a home security system from your company but is not happy with it. We are now threatening to take their case to the consumer watchdog and the industrial rights ombudsman. Your objective is to resolve the issue with the minimum damage to the company (both financially and in terms of reputation). Prepare your approach and plan to contact the client. "Sample role-play exercise 2–External Negotiation" You are a member of the team. The boss is the other role player. You have worked for this company for four years, working for your manager for the last two years. Work is very fun, but you get very little development time from the manager, and you're very happy to get on with it. The director will carry out the annual review with you every February. Lots of promises are made, but nothing seems to be done. There's always been a reason.

Samantha, who does a similar job for another supervisor, always seems to have a lot of time with him—analyzing results, taking intervention, various tasks, extra duty. She also spent a few weeks in another part of the organization on secondment.

You're determined to tackle this with your manager. It's just a chance to sit down with him / her. Your job is to persuade your boss to allow you more time to develop yourself. Make sure you get a firm commitment, such as the first' coaching' session in the diary. "These are very simple examples of two of the most common role-play scenarios. For highly detailed role-playing training and to master expert role-playing strategies, take a look at the Role-Play Masterclass.

'Ok, so we know what roleplay is and what employers want to see in the exercise. We've also seen some real-world briefs, so now is the moment to get into the nitty gritty. Let's look at the basics of how the role-plays center of interview and evaluation can succeed.

1) Read this summary carefully. Read the brief carefully, then.

This is absolutely crucial, as any misconceptions or misunderstandings that you make as you rush to start preparing can undermine all your subsequent efforts in this exercise. The role-plays described above are both quite basic, but the role-plays used for more senior selection can be extremely demanding and difficult.

You can fully understand what is expected of you during this exercise. What role are you being asked to play? Be absolutely clear on what you're being expected to do before you check it out.

I've lost count of the number of candidates I've seen go off on a redundant tangent because they haven't read the brief thoroughly enough—this obviously puts a black mark on your candidacy because it shows a lack of attention to detail.

So take a breath and make sure you fully understand the brief before you start preparing. Ask one of the assessors to explain, if possible. Some points are intentionally ambiguous, so just ask if you're sure they're not obvious.)

2) Prepare a list of open-ended questions.

Okay, this is massive. There's always a lot of information that isn't included in the document, and it's your responsibility to find and answer it. Questions that start like this are worth their weight in gold: "Tell me about..." "Can you expand on..." "Can you talk to me about..." Why are these questions so valuable? We send you the most important thing you're searching for in this exercise: more detail and transparency. In most role-plays, there are often a number of relevant and important specifics that are not included in the summary. Many specifics are deliberately omitted as this means that the role-play has a headroom to evolve and also allows the assessors to see if the applicant will think on their feet.

3) Plan the bookends are pre-prepared opening and closing sentences. Getting a pre-planned opening statement (just a few sentences) will help you calm down and relax in the test, as well as provide a positive first impression on the assessor.

Likewise, a strong closing statement will wrap things up well and leave a positive, long-lasting impression on you.

Spend a few moments while you're planning to build these. Attempt to commit them to memory, if they're too lengthy or too difficult to recall, then write them down in large-scale prose (so you can read them at a glance). Bookends bring a welcoming dimension of technical creativity to your success, so don't forget about it!

4) Plan a structural framework, but leave ALL Flexible Having a clear strategy before beginning a role-play exercise is necessary, but it's just as crucial that the experience happens as naturally as possible, so don't devise a predetermined plan and expect things to happen just as you've outlined on your piece of paper.

The dialogue should be allowed to flow wherever it wants to go, this is one of the key indicators of a role-play that's going well.

Why is versatility so important to us? Because your linear strategy could get out of the window at a moment's notice if the assessor throws a curve ball into the role-play activity (which they can and often will —particularly if you're doing well, just to see how you react).

One of the assessors tries to test how you adapt in unexpected circumstances, so keep things normal and comfortable to increase your chances of reacting well.

5) Have only 1 piece of paper on your desk / table This may sound small but it's a very practical point: don't have an impenetrable mess of planning and notes all over your lap or a scribbled piece of A4 of notes covering every inch of room. Only write bullet-points in a large size (i.e. easy to understand–even if you're nervous).

6) training, practicing, practicing Nothing will boost the day's success more than your experience with the workout. It will improve your competence and help you stay relaxed. You will perform comprehensive role-playing and experience a 45-minute training tutorial that brings you through your version of the ACHQ Expert Role-Play Training Framework

7) Be relaxed, natural & confident This is easy to say and difficult to do, but it is vital to your success. Read our post "How to Deal with Nerves & Panic" to know any

effective techniques to reduce any last minute panic. Remember, here you can get hold of a full suite of interview preparation tools.

How to Schedule a Last-Minute Interview in 30 Minutes

The hiring manager called, and he wants you to come in for an interview— this afternoon. You can change your plans around and tell your boss you've got an urgent dentist appointment, but in fact, you've just got 30 minutes to get ready.

Yeah, you might have talked about rescheduling (and for future reference, that's actually a good option), but in your excitement, you replied, "Certainly!" And requested an address from the HQ. So you know that calling back and asking to change the time is a no-no, because it lets it seem like you're unable to think on your feet.

Conclusion

Thank for making it through to the end of **Communication Skills**, let's hope it was informative and able to provide you with all of the tools you need to achieve your goals whatever they may be.

An interview is an essential aspect of applying for a job since it determines whether you get the job or not. While the applications you submitted shows your abilities and qualifications, the interview determines whether you are worthy of those qualities and how well you can perform in the role applied.

Job interview questions and modes of answering vary in different companies and sometimes, according to the interview. But what's most important in answering any company's interview question is your sincerity and enthusiasm to perform the job. Out of desperation to get the job, many candidates tell lies or give random answers, but the interviewer always knows who is perfect for the position.

However, the lists of 26 interview questions and answers have been provided to serve as a guide in achieving a successful interview. You may feel that some of the tips mentioned above may be unnecessary or won't make much difference, but the truth is your ability to answer or carry out these small tips has a significant impact on the interviews. That's why those little tips are essential.

www.ingramcontent.com/pod-product-compliance
Lightning Source LLC
Chambersburg PA
CBHW072007070526
44583CB00015B/1376